The Caste and Class Controversy on Race and Poverty

ROUND TWO OF THE WILLIE/WILSON DEBATE

SECOND EDITION

THE CASTE AND CLASS CONTROVERSY ON RACE AND POVERTY

ROUND TWO OF THE WILLIE/WILSON DEBATE

SECOND EDITION

Charles Vert Willie
Harvard University

GENERAL HALL, INC.
Publishers
5 Talon Way
Dix Hills, New York 11746

The Caste and Class Controversy on Race and Poverty

ROUND TWO OF THE WILLIE/WILSON DEBATE

SECOND EDITION

GENERAL HALL, INC.
5 Talon Way
Dix Hills, New York 11746

Publisher: Ravi Mehra
Composition: *Graphics Division,* General Hall, Inc.

LIBRARY OF CONGRESS CATALOG CARD NUMBER: 89-84677
ISBN: 0-930390-96-2 [paper]
      0-930390-97-0 [cloth]

Manufactured in the United States of America

This book is dedicated to the memory of

W. E. B. DuBois and E. Franklin Frazier

who identified race and social class
as the problems of the twentieth century

Contents

PREFACE TO FIRST EDITION

The summer of 1977 provided, for me, clear and present evidence that something is wrong with the way we analyze race relations in the United States. During the first week in September of that year William J. Wilson, a black professor of sociology at the University of Chicago, presented a lecture at the annual meeting of the prestigious Sociological Research Association and told that group that social class has become more important than race in determining access to economic power and privileges for blacks in the United States. This conclusion later was included in his book *The Declining Significance of Race* that was published in 1978. Further, he said that the rate of entry into positions of influence and prestige by blacks who are educated and have talent, in some instances, is greater than that for whites with similar qualifications.

Less than two weeks before Professor Wilson delivered his treatise on "The Declining Significance of Race," The *New York Times* (August 29, 1977, p. C35) published the report of an interview with Sanford Allen, a black violinist with the New York Philharmonic, who announced his intention to resign from his position with that prestigious organization. He said he was "simply tired of being a symbol." At that time Allen was the only black who had been a member of that orchestra that was more than one and one-third centuries old. He charged the more influential and prestigious symphony orchestras of this nation, such as the Boston Symphony, the Chicago Symphony and two or three others with running a closed shop that has resulted in black exclusion. Allen said he often got telephone calls from good, black musicians who had heard about a philharmonic audition coming up. When they asked, "Is there really any point in coming," the black violinist said he was not always sure how to

1

answer that question, since he then was the only black member of the orchestra that he joined in 1962; during a decade and a half, no other blacks had been hired. The Allen experience did not fit well with the Wilson pronouncement.

Finally, as the summer of 1977 drew near the end, a nation-wide Harris Survey revealed that 48 percent of the blacks believed their progress had been "too slow" while 55 percent of the whites thought that black people had tried to "move too fast" in achieving racial equality. Moreover, nearly three-fifths of the population believed that the black executive of the National Urban League was not justified in publicly criticizing the President of the United States for "neglecting blacks, the poor and other minorities" (*Boston Globe,* September 12, 1977).

Meanwhile, the Census Bureau reported that the number of blacks enrolled in college during the Bicentennial Year was 1.1 million, that this number represented more than a three-fold increase in one decade and that about 7 percent of all blacks were college graduates, representing approximately a two-fold increase in one decade.

Also during the summer of 1977, arguments — pro and con — raged over radio, television, and in magazines and newspapers concerning whether these educated blacks could continue their education in graduate professional schools such as medical schools. The issue was whether spaces could be reserved in entering classes for minorities who might not otherwise be admitted because of the effects of previous discrimination. Some claimed that quotas for blacks were unfair to whites. Others said that this was the only method that was just for all.

These many different issues, contrasting views, and contradictory themes that issued forth during the summer of 1977 indicated that if race was declining in significance for some people, it was increasing in significance for others. A problem with our analysis of race relations is that the focus usually is too narrow.

Any analysis of black gains or losses must also determine the significance of these for whites and vice versa. A comparative or comprehensive analysis that focuses on all is necessary because the majority and minority are linked together in the United States in a symbiotic relationship metaphorically labeled by Anthropologist Stanley Diamond as "a hellish minuet" (Diamond, *Dissent,* Autumn 1965, p. 474). I arrived at a similar conclusion after studying the case histories of twelve black middle-class, working-class, and lower-class families. On the basis of that analysis, I concluded "[1] that black and white families in America share a common core of values, [2] that they adapt to the society and its values in different ways, largely because of racial discrimination, and [3] that the unique adaptation of blacks is further differentiated by variations in style of life by social class. Any assumption that the life of blacks in America can be understood independent of their involvement with whites appears to be unwarranted" (Willie, *A New Look at Black Families, 1976,* p. 195).

Blacks have seen their population differentiate in a short period of time from a more or less homogeneous category of poor people, of whom less than one-eighth was middle class as late as the mid-twentieth century, according to E. Franklin Frazier (Frazier, *The Negro Family in Chicago*), to the last quarter of this 100-year span in which about one-third of the black population is middle-class or higher.

If one were to analyze black gains from an affirmative action perspective and interpret them as white losses, then Wilson could have used the same set of data but carried the title "The Increasing Significance of Race for Whites." Indeed whites have seen their authority and power eroded over the years from the age of slavery when blacks were totally under their control and were of little, if any, competition to the present time when courts of law are rendering decisions in favor of black plaintiffs and against white defendants and are requiring remedies to redress past grievances and the payment of penalties for damages that resulted from deliberate efforts on the part of whites to harm blacks. For whites, who must adapt to and abide by court orders that favor blacks, race clearly is a salient feature that encroaches upon their previous way of life.

The turbulence in community life today because of court-ordered school desegregation and the dither of some whites about affirmative action goals, practices, and procedures indicate that race is very much salient for whites and appears to be increasing rather than decreasing in significance. The national interest generated by the Bakke case that alleged "reverse discrimination" is indicative of the saliency of race to many whites.

W. E. B. DuBois said that the problem of the twentieth century would be that of color and E. Franklin Frazier said that social stratification is the most significant frame of reference for studying social change in community life. Together, these two social scientists identified the issues of this age that are shaking the foundation of this nation— race and social class.

Wherever these two parameters are found, there is the tension of inequality. Whenever these two parameters intersect, there is a compounded tension of inequality; together, caste and class are explosive. William Wilson's book *The Declining Significance of Race* focused on the agony that racial and socio-economic inequality have generated in a society where justice is significant and contributed to a minor explosion.

The analysis in this book demonstrates why many have been swift to reject the Wilson hypothesis that social class is a more significant determinant of life chances than race in the United States at this period in its history. At stake is the continued implementation of affirmative action plans and antidiscrimination programs.

Part I of this book lays out alternative interpretations and comes to the conclusion that institutional oppression due to elitism as well as racism is alive and well in America. This conclusion is based on a review of research in which the author has been engaged for more than a quarter of a century. Also, Part I presents a theoretical discussion of class, status, and race in the system of social stratification in the United States. It presents the author's own understanding of these concepts based on a variety of experiences in research and policy matters and includes some of the material used in his debate with Wilson at Michigan State University in November of 1978 and at the Eastern Sociological Society in March 1979.

Part II consists of analytical comments by other social scientists. Three book reviews, original essays, and an excerpt from a National Urban League report are included.

The Summary and Conclusion consist of commentaries prepared by the author and William J. Wilson for the 1978 July/ August issue of *Society* magazine and the statement issued by the Association of Black Sociologists. Appreciation is expressed to *Contemporary Sociology, Social Forces, Change* magazine, *Society,* the Research Division of the National Urban League, and the *Washington Post* for permission to reprint material that they had published.

If a controversy is the creative kernel of history and truth has a better chance of emerging from controversy, this book is offered as a contribution to that truth which is always partial until confronted by another version.

C.V.W.
Harvard University
Cambridge, Massachusetts
August, 1979

PREFACE TO SECOND EDITION

The preface to the first edition carried a *New York Times* story about the alleged discrimination against black musicians by major symphony orchestras in the United States. A dozen years later the race relations climate for black professionals and black musicians, in particular, had not changed substantially. March 5, 1989, the *New York Times* reported that the Detroit Symphony Orchestra hired the first black musician it has hired in fourteen years. However, this action was taken only after several state legislators threatened to withhold more than a million dollars in state aid and to boycott and picket the orchestra's concerts if the orchestra did not hire more blacks (p. 1).

Also, as the 1980s came to a close, discrimination against other black professionals was revealed. In Atlanta, Georgia, a black college professor, who is an elected public official, had a mortgage loan application rejected by two white-owned banks despite his family income of nearly $100,000 because he wanted to purchase a house in a minority neighborhood.

The black musicians were competent professionals and the black professor/public official was a worthy borrower. Nevertheless, they were rejected or had difficulty being accepted because of racial prejudice. Their experiences indicate that race continues as a criterion for offering or withdrawing opportunities to individuals in the United States. Affluent as well as poor blacks, educated as well as ignorant blacks, and competent as well as unskilled blacks are truly disadvantaged.

A poll conducted by Louis Harris for the NAACP Legal Defense in 1988 revealed some ways in which blacks are disadvantaged. According to survey findings, a substantial proportion of whites hold rigid stereotypes about all blacks and believe that they have less ambition than people affiliated with the majority population. Based on this and other data, Harris declared that blacks and whites are worlds apart in their perception of race relations in the United States (*The New York Times,* January 12, 1989, p. 7).

Clearly, justice has not been fully achieved. This is bad news in a democratic nation-state. However, attacking those who bring the bad news will not solve the problem of injustice. What is needed is a proper analysis of both how and why a wealthy nation is not generous, hoards its resources, and will not share them with its citizens who are poor. Also needed is a proper analysis of how and why a society dominated by whites is not compassionate and has a need to continue to oppress its minority members. Many investigations have focused on what blacks and whites do and how they behave but few have attempted to understand why these populations follow certain courses of action.

To help clarify the issues mentioned, this book is offered as a continuation of the Willie/Wilson debate that has been in progress for more than a decade. Another round of the debate is necessary now that Wilson's book, *The Truly Disadvantaged* (1987) has been published. It reveals that Wilson neither understands the value of comparative analysis nor the principle of redress. Indeed, one could classify Wilson's action strategy for dealing with poverty that rejects population-specific remedies as flawed.

This book retains the initial material of the debate that appeared in separate articles published in *Society* magazine in 1978 and included in the first edition. Also retained is the analytical commentary on *The Declining Significance of Race* (1978) that was prepared by Richard Margolis, Harry Edwards, Thomas Pettigrew, and Thomas Payne and published in the first edition. New chapters have been added on alternative perspectives on race and social class, the significance of race in the United States over a three-decade period, and the cure and prevention of poverty and racism. Commentaries on *The Truly Disadvantaged* (1987) prepared by Theodore Lowi, Harold Rose, and the author have been included for the first time in this edition.

Acknowledged with appreciation is the *Public Policies Review* which gave permission for three book reviews of Wilson's 1987 volume to be reprinted in this edition. Also acknowledged with thanks is General Hall which permitted material originally published in *Race, Ethnicity and Socio-economic Status* (1983) to be included in this book as Chapter 3 and material originally published in *A New Look at Black Families* (1976), (1981), (1988) to be included in this edition as Chapters 4, 5 and 6, respectively. Acknowledged with appreciation is a grant from the Maurice Falk Medical Fund which supported the preparation of this second edition.

C.V.W.
Harvard University
Cambridge, Massachusetts
August, 1989

PART I

THE DEBATE

Chapter **1** THE INCLINING
SIGNIFICANCE OF RACE*

Charles V. Willie

Commentary prepared for *Society* magazine, July/August 1978,
in response to an excerpt from *The Declining Significance of Race*
by William J. Wilson that was published in the January/February
issue.

It is all a matter of perspective. From the perspective of the
dominant people of power, inequality exists because of the personal inadequacies of those who are less fortunate. Varying
degrees of fortune is the essence of the social stratification
system in this nation. In America, it is the affluent rather than
the poor who use social class theory to explain poverty. Moreover,
they assert that poverty is not a function of institutional arrangements but a matter of individual capacities. From the perspective of the dominant people of power, the social stratification
system in the United States is open and anyone who has the
capacity can rise within it. This orientation toward individual
mobility tends to mask the presence of opportunities that are in-
stitutionally based such as attending the "right" school, seeking
employment with the "right" company or firm, and being of the
"right" race. Also this orientation toward individual mobility
tends to deny the presence of opposition and oppression that are
connected with institutions. According to the perspective of the
dominant people of power, opportunity and especially educational and economic opportunity is a function of merit.

William Julius Wilson has used the perspective of the dominant people of power in his article on "The Declining Significance Of Race" that appeared in the January/February edition of *Society*. An individual, including a scholar in the social sciences, is free to use any perspective that he or she wishes to use. The tradition of friendly criticism in this field, however, supports the effort which I shall undertake in this commentary. My purpose is to make explicit that which is implicit so that others may assess the conclusions of Professor Wilson on the basis of the premises and the perspective of his analysis.

At the end of his article which asserts that "Class has become more important than race in determining black life chances in the modern industrial period," Professor Wilson tries to disassociate himself from individualism of the dominant people of power by calling for "public policy programs to attack inequality on a broad class front — policy programs, in other words, that go beyond the limits of ethnic and racial discrimination by directly confronting the pervasive and destructive features of class subordination." The action which Professor Wilson calls for ignores the interconnection between race and social class as a complex of interrelated characteristics and further does not take cognizance of the fact that there may be a serial pattern to the solution to social problems.

COMPLEX OF CHARACTERISTICS

An historic example is given. One reason other scholars did not discover the laws of population genetics before Mendel is that "they treated as units the complexes of characteristics of individuals, races and species and attempted to find rules governing inheritance of such complexes," according to Theodosius Dobzhansky. "Mendel was the first to understand that ... the inheritance of separate traits [and] not [the inheritance of] complexes of traits ... had to be studied." With reference to the community and processes of social change, Susan Greenblatt and I have pointed out in an article entitled, "A New Approach To Comparative Community Analysis" that maybe it is the other way around. "It is possible that we may successfully understand school desegregation [or poverty and race relations] by using a method that analyzes complexes of characteristics." Professor Wilson attempts to analyze the relationships between the races in the United States in terms of individual traits rather than as a complex of characteristics. The traits in which he is most interested have to do with the economy. Professor Wilson acknowledges that "in the modern industrial period race relations have been shaped as much by important economic changes as by important political changes," but then he denies the significance of this complex by stating the following: "... ingenious schemes of racial exploitation, discrimination and segregation ... however significant they were in the creation of poverty-stricken ghettos and a vast under-class of black proletarians ... do not provide a meaningful explanation of the life chances of black Americans today." He goes on to say that the significance of the association between "race and economic class only" has grown as the nation has entered the modern industrial period.

While making this assertion, Professor Wilson acknowledges that "the presence of blacks is still firmly resisted in various institutions and social arrangements, for example, residential areas and private social clubs." By attempting to isolate the economic sphere from the other institutions and social arrangements of society, Professor Wilson has committed the error of particularism, an error committed by many social scientists who attempt to model analysis of the social system after the organic system, who attempt to analyze traits rather than the complex of characteristics. Evidence from other studies have demonstrated an association between economic opportunity, educational opportunity, and residential location. This is what the current movement for school desegregation and the resistance to busing are all about. Thus, resistance to the presence of blacks in residential areas, for example, cannot be dismissed as irrelevant to social mobility in the economic sphere.

My own study of the "Relative Contribution Of Family Status And Economic Status To Juvenile Delinquency" that was published in *Social Problems* in 1967 illuminates the serial approach to the solution of social problems. In summary, I found: "In Washington, D.C., 80 percent of the white population lives in economically affluent areas while 67 percent of the non-white population lives in neighborhoods of poverty or marginal economic condition. Since poverty was no longer an overwhelming problem for most white people, family instability was a major remaining and outstanding problem contributing to the incidence of juvenile delinquency. Although the percent of non-white children growing up in one-parent families was greater than the percent of white children who had this kind of experience, the impoverished economic circumstances of non-whites was overwhelming. In the light of the data ... [I] hypothesized that non-whites may be able to deal with the family instability factor which is associated with juvenile delinquency only after notable improvements have been experienced in their economic circumstances. The hypothesis is advanced on the basis of the findings ... pertaining to the white population which is largely beyond the pale of poverty."

SERIAL PATTERN

Out of this analysis I developed the principle that the solutions of some social problems occur in a serial pattern, that the solution to one problem makes possible the solution of another. There is an ordering of social events into a sequential pattern. Most whites have passed beyond the stage of economic insecurity. Thus strengthening their families is the most significant way to further reduce delinquency in the white population. But efforts to strengthen family ties and increase family stability among blacks probably will not be very successful until opportunities for economic upgrading are provided. This assertion was based on the findings that 40 percent of the variance in the family instability factor could be attributed to socioeconomic status at that time in Washington.

Thus, I concluded that "this society may have the possibility of helping a population achieve greater family stability ... only after it has assisted a population to achieve greater economic security."* Not only are most social problems a complex of characteristics such as that of juvenile delinquency, socioeconomic status, and race, but also their solution must be approached in a sequential way. Clearly the public policy of strengthening the black family as a way of overcoming various forms of pathology that was advocated by Daniel Patrick Moynihan, first, was a projection most appropriate for whites upon blacks and, second, was a violation of the sequential approach to social problem solving. Neither social scientists nor public policymakers are free to pick and choose points of intervention that they prefer, if they wish to be effective. Professor Wilson, for example, may wish to focus on the economic sphere and social class as a way of dealing with inequality. But racial discrimination and oppression in "various institutions and social arrangements" may require intervention in these areas first.

Professor Wilson suggests that changes in many spheres, other than economic, already have occurred in previous stages which he has designated as stage one, the Plantation Economy and Racial/Caste Oppression; stage two, Industrial Expansion, Class Conflict and Racial Oppression; and stage three, during the 1960s and 1970s, Progressive Transition from Race Inequalities to Class Inequality. My contention is that the transition is far from complete for upper-class, middle-class, working-class, and under-class blacks and that barriers to economic opportunity still are largely a function of discrimination based on race and sex.

The remainder of this discussion will demonstrate this fact with data and point out errors in the analysis of William Julius Wilson that may be a function of the perspective used that probably caused him to miss some essential information.

INCOME

First, let us look at income. As recently as 1975, the median income for white families was $14,268 compared with a median

---

*I did not state explicitly the connection between economic insecurity and racial discrimination in this commentary. I assumed that it was self-evident. However, Wilson's response to this commentary indicates that what was implicit should have been made explicit.

of $9,321 for blacks and other minority races. This means that blacks and other racial minorities received only two-thirds as much income as did whites. At both ends of the income scale, the ratio of black to white income was about the same. Under $5,000 a year, there was only 10.2 percent of the white families and individuals compared with 26.3 percent of the population of black families and individuals. Earning $25,000 a year and over in 1975 was 15.1 percent of the white population compared wtih 6.4 percent of the black population. The proportion of blacks who were very poor was two and one-half times greater than the proportion of whites who were very poor; and the proportion of whites who were most affluent was two and one-third times greater than the proportion of blacks with high incomes. There is not much of a difference in these income ratios by race for the poor and the affluent. In general, the proportion of high income blacks is far less than what it would be if there was no racial discrimination. The 1977 report, *All Our Children,* by the Carnegie Council on Children of which Kenneth Keniston was senior author states that "90 percent of the income gap between blacks and whites is the result ... of lower pay for blacks with comparable levels of education and experience." Despite this and other findings such as those presented by economist Herman Miller in his book *Rich Man, Poor Man,* Professor Wilson states that "many talented and educated blacks are now entering positions of prestige and influence at a rate comparable to or, in some situations, exceeding that of whites with equal qualifications."

In 1974, 15 percent of the white male population was of the professional or technical worker category compared with 9 percent of the male population of blacks and other minority races. This appeared to be a notable change relative to whites but it represented only an increase of 3 percentage points over the 6 percent of black and other minority males who were professionals ten years earlier. Moreover, only 5 percent of the black and other racial minority males were managers and administrators in 1974 compared with 15 percent of all white employed males. In summary, 42 percent of the white male population was white collar in 1974 compared with 24 percent of the racial minority males in this nation. These data indicate that blacks have a long way to go before they catch up with whites in high-level occupations.

Moreover, a study by the Survey Research Center of the University of Michigan that was published in the *New York Times,* February 26, 1978, reported that 61 percent of all blacks in a nationwide poll believed that whites either do not care whether or not blacks "get a break" or were actively trying to keep blacks down. It would appear that neither the sentiment of blacks nor the facts of the situation are in accord with the analysis of Professor Wilson and his claim that "class has become more important than race in determining black life chances."

The University of Michigan study also found that one out of every two white persons believed that "few blacks ... miss out on jobs and promotions because of racial discrimination." This response is similar to the conclusion of Professor Wilson and is the reason why I stated earlier that his analysis was from the perspective of the dominant people of power.

EDUCATION

Second, let us look at what is happening to poor blacks to determine whether their circumstances are more a function of social class than of race. This analysis, I believe, reveals a fundamental error in the analysis of Professor Wilson — an error no less serious than that committed by Daniel Patrick Moynihan and Christopher Jencks who made observations on whites and projected these upon blacks. Howard Taylor, a sociologist and expert methodologist, has stated that Jencks took "considerable liberties in discussing the effects of integration, segregation, race, etc., upon occupational and income inequality. He clearly infers that education is not related to success for black people; that if blacks want more money, then more education will not get it. But this inference is based upon path analysis done only on native white, non-farm males who took the armed forces IQ test! Who can say that causal models and estimates based on native white, non-farm males are applicable to blacks? Not one single path analysis in the entire report is performed on even one black sample." Howard Taylor made these observations in an article entitled "Playing The Dozens With Path Analysis" that was published by the *Sociology of Education* in 1973.

It is obvious that Professor Wilson has analyzed the job situation for affluent blacks. The census data that I reported earlier indicated that blacks were catching up with whites, relatively, so far as employment in the professions is concerned. While the proportion of white male professionals a decade ago was twice as great as the proportion of black and other minority male professionals, the proportion as late as 1974 was only two-thirds greater. On the basis of data like these, Professor Wilson states that "talented and educated blacks are experiencing unprecedented job opportunities in the growing government and corporate sectors." After analyzing the "job situation for the more privileged blacks," Professor Wilson projects these findings upon the poor and says, "it would be difficult to argue that the plight of the black under-class is solely the consequence of racial oppression, that is, the explicit and overt efforts of whites to keep blacks subjugated...."

While the facts cited earlier cast doubt upon the conclusion that talented blacks are experiencing "unprecedented job opportunities," even if one accepts the modest improvement for "talented blacks" as fact, it is inappropriate to project middle-class experience upon the under-class of blacks. This is precisely what Professor Wilson has done.

His assertion that "the black experience has moved historically from economic racial oppression experienced by virtually all blacks to economic subordination for the black under-class" cancels out racial discrimination as a key cause of poverty among blacks. If one assumes that there are not extraordinary biological differences between blacks and whites in the United States, then it is difficult to explain why the proportion of poor blacks with an annual income under $5,000 is two and one-half times greater than the proportion of poor whites. Among poor white youth and young adults, the unemployment rate is higher for high school dropouts than for persons who graduated from high school but did not receive more education. Among blacks, however, the unemployment rate is high and is the same for high school dropouts and for those who graduated from high school but did not receive more education. Staying in high school seems not to make a difference for blacks so far as the risk of unemployment is concerned.

Among whites with only an elementary school education or less, 50 percent are likely to have jobs as service workers or laborers at the bottom of the occupational heap; but 80 percent of black workers with this limited education are likely to find work only in these kinds of jobs. This was what Herman Miller found in his analysis of 1960 census data. These facts indicate that education alone cannot explain the disproportionate number of blacks in low-paying jobs. If the absence of education is the basis for limited upward mobility in the stratification system, why do whites with little education get better jobs than blacks?

Using 1968 data, Miller analyzed the difference in median income for whites and blacks and other non-white minorities. He found that the difference for the races ranged from $880 for those who had completed grade school only to $2,469 for those who had attended or graduated from college. Median income by schooling not only differed by race but tended to widen between the racial groups with increase in education. On the bases of these findings, Miller said that "there is some justification for the feeling by Puerto Ricans, Negroes and other minoritiy groups that education does not do as much for them financially as it does for others." These findings Miller reported in the 1971 edition of his book, *Rich Man, Poor Man,* and they indicated that racial discrimination is a contributing factor to the occupational opportunities and income received by poor as well as affluent blacks.

RESIDENTIAL SEGREGATION

With reference to residential segregation which Professor Wilson wants to ignore as irrelevant, he has received modest support from the findings of Albert Simkus that were reported in the February 1978 edition of the *American Sociological Review* in an article entitled "Residential Segregation By Occupation And Race in Ten Urbanized Areas, 1950–1970." Simkus said that "historically, blacks with high incomes have been as highly or more highly segregated from whites with similar incomes than have low-income blacks." This fact became "slightly less true ... by 1970." However, Simkus attributes the slight change to political rather than economic factors. Particularly singled out for credit is civil rights and housing legislation of the 1960s.

Simkus points out that the decrease in residential segregation of affluent blacks is beginning to catch up with the integrated residential areas that characterized lower-income blacks and whites in the past. Specifically, he said that "apart from the comparisons involving non-white professionals, non-whites and whites in the lowest occupational categories were still slightly less segregated than those in the higher categories."

Finally, I call attention to the fact that Professor Wilson's data are at variance with the clinical observations of other blacks. The unprecedented job opportunities simply have not been experienced by some talented and educated blacks. During the summer of 1977, the *New York Times* published an interview with Sanford Allen, a black violinist with the New York Philharmonic Orchestra. Allen announced his intention to resign from his position. He said that he was "simply tired of being a symbol." At that time, Allen was the only black who had been a member of the 133-year-old musical organization. He charged the more prestigious symphony orchestras of this nation, such as the Boston Symphony, the Chicago Symphony, and two or three others with running a closed shop that excluded blacks. Allen joined the New York Philharmonic in 1962. During a decade and a half, no other blacks had been hired. A story like this one, of course, is clinical evidence and does not carry the same weight as research evidence systematically gathered. But such clinical evidence has been accumulating recently and deserves to be looked at carefully.

The response of white professionals to admissions policies by colleges and universities that are designed to reserve spaces for members of previously excluded racial populations in the first-year classes of professional schools is a case in point. The opposition to such practices indicates that talented and educated blacks are not being given access to privilege and power "at a rate comparable to or in some situations, exceeding that of whites with equivalent qualifications" as Professor Wilson claims. The opposition to special minority admissions programs is led by white professionals, not white hard-hat or blue-collar workers. This is further clinical evidence that race is not irrelevant and has not declined in significance for talented and educated blacks.

COUNTERHYPOTHESIS

Actually, I would like to introduce a counterhypothesis that the significance of race is increasing and that it is increasing especially for middle-class blacks who, because of school desegregation and affirmative action and other integration programs, are coming into direct contact with whites for the first time for extended interaction.

My case studies of black families, who have moved into racially integrated neighborhoods and racially integrated work situations, indicate that race for some of these pioneers is a consuming experience. They seldom can get away from it. When special opportunities are created, such as in the admissions programs, the minorities who take advantage of them must constantly prove themselves. When a middle-class black has been accepted as Sanford Allen was in the Philharmonic, the issue then shifts to whether or not one is being used as a symbol. Try as hard as they may, middle-class blacks, especially middle-class blacks in racially integrated situations at this period in American history, are almost obsessed with race. Many have experienced this adaptation especially in residential and work situations.

Any obsession, including obsession with race, is painful. Freedom is circumscribed and options are delimited not because of physical segregation but because of the psychological situation.

So painful is the experience of racial obsession that two extreme reactions are likely to occur. Middle-class blacks may attempt to deal with the obsession by capitulation — that is, by assuming everything is race-related, that all whites are racists, and that all events and circumstances must be evaluated first in terms of their racial implications. The other adaptation is denial, believing that race is irrelevant and insignificant even when there is clear and present evidence that it is not. This is one of the personal consequences of a racist society for the oppressed as the old separatist system begins to crumble. The people who most severely experience the pain of dislocation due to the changing times are the racial minorities who are talented and educated and integrated, not those who are impoverished and isolated.

READINGS SUGGESTED BY THE AUTHOR

Blau, Peter M. 1977. *Inequality and Heterogeneity.* New York: Free Press.

Miller, Herman. 1964. *Rich Man, Poor Man.* New York: Thomas Crowell.

Simkus, Albert. "Residential Segregation by Occupation and Race in Ten Urbanized Areas, 1950–1970." *American Sociological Review 43* (February 1978): 81–93.

Taylor, Howard F., "Playing the Dozens with Path Analysis." *Sociology of Education* 46 (Fall 1973): 433–50.

Willie, Charles V. 1988. *A New Look at Black Families.* Dix Hills, N.Y.: General Hall.

Chapter **2** THE DECLINING
SIGNIFICANCE OF RACE
Revisited But Not Revised*

William Julius Wilson

Rejoinder prepared for *Society* magazine, July/August 1978 in response to the commentary by Charles V. Willie about the excerpt from *The Declining Significance of Race* that was published in the January/February 1978 issue.

Professor Charles V. Willie says that it is all a matter of perspective. He is wrong, it is also a matter of interpretation. And his interpretation of the excerpts from my book (*Society,* January/February 1978), *The Declining Significance of Race,* erroneously associates what is, in fact, a macro-sociological argument of inequality with a so-called dominant group perspective of individual mobility.

In my response to Willie's contentions I do not plan to devote much attention to perspectives; the reader can easily make that judgment. Instead, the bulk of this paper will consider the validity of assertions. In the process I hope to demonstrate that, under close scrutiny, not a single one of Willie's "empirical" criticisms can be upheld, and that contrary to his claims, the data he presents and the counterhypotheses he proposed neither demonstrate errors in my analysis nor undermine my arguments on the growing importance of class and the decreasing significance of race in determining blacks' chances in life.

*Published by permission of Transaction Publishers, from *Society*, Vol. 15, No. 5. Copyright © 1978 by Transaction Publishers.

MACRO-SOCIOLOGICAL ANALYSIS
OF RACE AND CLASS

However, before I directly comment on Willie's article, I would like, in a few succinct paragraphs, to put the basic arguments of my book in proper focus. My book is an attempt to explain race and class in the American experience. I feel that in order to understand the changing issues of race and, indeed, the relationship between class and race in America, a framework that would relate changes in intergroup relations with changes in the American social structure is required. Individual mobility is not used as the independent variable in explaining race and class experiences, as Willie's analysis would suggest. Rather I try to show how the economy and state interacted in different historical periods not only to structure the relations between blacks and whites and to produce dissimilar contexts for the manifestation of racial antagonisms, but also to create different situations for racial-group access to rewards and privileges. Using this framework, I define three stages of American race relations (the preindustrial, industrial, and modern industrial), stages in which I describe the role of both the system of production and the state in the development of race and class relations.

Although my book devotes considerable attention to the preindustrial and industrial periods of American race relations, it is my description of the modern industrial period that has generated controversy and has provoked Willie to respond. I contend that in the earlier periods, whether one focuses on the way race relations were structured by the economy or by the state or both, racial oppression (ranging from the exploitation of black labor by the economic elite to the elimination of black competition, especially economic competition, by the white masses) was a characteristic and important aspect of life. However, I also maintain that in the modern industrial period the economy and the state have, in relatively independent ways, shifted the basis of racial antagonisms away from the black/white economic contact to social, political, and community issues. The net effect is a growing class division among blacks, a situation, in other words, in which economic class has been elevated to a position of greater importance than race in determining individual black opportunities for living conditions and personal life experiences.

Now, it is difficult to recapture in these few paragraphs the distinctions and arguments presented in *The Declining Significance of Race,* but the preceding synopsis will at least provide the necessary background in considering Willie's interpretation and critique of my thesis.

WILLIE'S ANALYSIS

In fairness to Willie, it should be pointed out that he was responding to the excerpts from my book that appeared in *Society* magazine and, therefore, did not have the benefit of the full array of data and arguments I use to support my contentions. I will therefore discuss some of these data in the ensuing paragraphs, as well as present some additional facts that were not incorporated in *The Declining Significance of Race* but which serve to demonstrate the inadequacies of Professor Willie's data.

Willie presents three major arguments: (1) that I "commit the error of particularism" in the sense that I try "to isolate the economic sphere from the other institutions and social arrangements of society;" (2) that barriers to economic opportunities for blacks are still mainly a function of race and that the available data support this contention; and (3) that a counter-hypothesis should be proposed, namely that "the significance of race is increasing ... especially for middle-class blacks who, because of school desegregation and affirmative action and other integration programs, are coming into direct contact with whites for the first time for extended interactions."

ERROR OF PARTICULARISM

In response to Willie's charge that I "isolate the economic sphere from the other institutions and social arrangements of society," let me say, first of all, that I would be the last to deny that there is an empirical "association between economic opportunity, educational opportunity, and residential location." Indeed, contrary to Willie's assertion, this complex relationship is demonstrated repeatedly in several chapters of my book. The problem has to do with the direction of the relationship. What I attempt to show is that in the modern industrial period, as economic opportunity for blacks increasingly depends on class affiliation, we see corresponding differences in black educational opportunity and residential location. Thus as the black middle class experiences greater occupational mobility, they, like more privileged whites, abandon public schools and send their children to private schools. Accordingly, public schools in large urban areas are not only suffering from racial isolation: they are also suffering from class isolation. By the same token, higher-income blacks are not trapped in depressed ghettos and, although they have greater difficulty than middle-class whites in finding housing, their economic resources provide them with more opportunities to find desirable housing and neighborhoods either in the central city or in the suburbs than both lower-income blacks and lower-income whites. On the other hand, the lack of economic opportunity for under-class blacks means that they are forced to attend inferior ghetto schools and remain in economically depressed ghettos. Ghetto isolation and inferior educational opportunities reinforce their low position in the labor market. This process is a vicious circle and, to repeat, is demonstrated in my book, even though I give more weight to economic opportunities than to noneconomic opportunities.

Furthermore, I agree with Willie's assertion that "efforts to strengthen family ties and increase family stability among blacks probably will not be very successful until opportunities for economic upgrading are provided." Indeed, this is one of the major arguments of chapter six of *The Declining Significance of Race*. For example, I show that in 1974 only 18 percent of the children in black families with incomes of less than $4,000 lived with both parents while 90 percent of the children in black families of $15,000 or more lived with both parents. I argue, therefore, that "to suggest categorically that the problem of female-headed households is characteristic of black families is to overlook the powerful influence of economic-class background. The increase in female-headed households among poor blacks is a consequence of the fact that the poorly trained and educated black males have increasingly restricted opportunities for higher-paying jobs and, thus, find it increasingly difficult to satisfy the expectations of being a male breadwinner." If Willie and I do have a real difference of opinion on this matter, it is that he associates the increasing difficulties of the black poor with racial discrimination whereas I maintain (and will further elaborate below) that class restrictions associated with structural shifts in the economy are the more important factors in accounting for poor blacks' limited occupational mobility today.

But Willie is not always consistent in his arguments about the "sequential approach to social problem solving." On the one hand he argues, as, in fact, I do, that efforts to strengthen black families will not succeed until economic opportunities are upgraded; yet, on the other hand, he contradicts this position with the statement that "Professor Wilson, for example, may wish to focus on the economic sphere and social class as a way of dealing with inequality. But racial discrimination and oppression in 'various institutions and social arrangements' may require intervention in these areas first." I stand by my contention that the factors that most severely affected black life chances in previous years were racial oppression and antagonism in the economic sector. As race declined in importance in the economic sector, the black class structure became more differentiated and black life chances increasingly became a consequence of class affiliation. This is not to deny the importance of racial antagonism in the social-political order, or even to suggest that residential, social, and educational discrimination do not form a part of a vicious circle that feeds back to the economic sector. But this circular process is far more relevant for poor blacks than for more privileged blacks. In terms of understanding life chances, the economic mobility of privileged blacks has offset the negative consequences of racial discrimination in the social-political order. Indeed, one will only be able to understand the growing class divisions in the black community by recognizing that racial antagonisms in the sociopolitical order have far less effect on black individual or group access to those opportunities and resources that are centrally important for life chances than have racial antagonisms in the economic sector.

But the bulk of Willie's article concentrates on data he presents to "point out errors" in my analysis. I would now like to examine these data and Willie's interpretation of them.

In an attempt to refute my assertion that class has become more significant than race in determining black life chances, Willie presents data indicating (1) that the median income for black families in 1975 was several thousand dollars less than the median income for white families; (2) that the proportion of black families who were poor (income of less than $5,000 a year) was two and one-half times greater than the proportion of white families who were poor and the proportion of white families who were affluent (income of $25,000 or more a year) was two and one-third times greater than the proportion of black families who were affluent; (3) that 90 percent of the black-white income gap is the result of lower pay for blacks with comparable experience and education; (4) that in 1968 "median income by schooling not only differed by race but tended to widen between the racial groups with increase in education;" (5) that staying in high school for blacks does not make a difference with respect to the risk of unemployment; and (6) that "42 percent of the white male population was white-collar in 1974 compared with 24 percent of racial minority members in the nation."

The problem with these statistics is not that they are inaccurate or even that some are outdated. The problem is that they obscure the very important distinction between the effects of past discrimination and the current effects of race in the economic world. In other words, they allow investigators to either ignore or overlook the importance of a legacy of past discrimination and, therefore, to interpret the overall black-white gap in income and employment as an indication of present discrimination. The fact that this approach tends to distort the significance of race today is most clearly revealed when we examine the labor market experiences of various subgroups within the black population.

BLACK EDUCATED MALES

There is compelling evidence that young black male college graduates now receive roughly the same salaries as young white men with college degrees. Data from the 1970 Census of Population show that in 1969 black male graduates age twenty-two to twenty-four received a slightly higher average income than comparable whites; and more recent findings from the 1973 *Current Population Survey* show that black men with college degrees in the twenty-five to twenty-nine age category earned close to $1,000 more than their white counterparts. Moreover, the economist Richard B. Freeman found that the starting salaries of male graduates from black colleges in the South in 1968-70 were comparable to the average starting salaries for male college graduates on a national level. These findings, obscured in Willie's gross income comparisons of all college-educated blacks and all college-educated whites, represent a significant change from the discriminatory pattern of the past whereby black college graduates at all age levels received substantially lower salaries than white college graduates of comparable ages.

But why have young black male college graduates finally reached income parity with young white male college graduates? Because the combination of an increased demand for white-collar salaried employees in the corporate and government sector and the pressures of state antidiscrimination programs, especially affirmative action pressures, have cleared the path for minority college graduates and have allowed them to enter positions of prestige and influence denied to them in the past. We only need to examine the changing racial practices of corporations to see that opportunities for educated blacks have sharply increased. As shown in Freeman's study, the efforts of corporations to recruit college-trained blacks increased sharply between 1965 and 1970. In fact, the average number of recruitment visits of representatives of corporations to predominantly black colleges rose from 4 in 1960 to 50 in 1965 and then climbed to 297 in 1970. And schools such as Clark College, Atlanta University, and Southern University, to which no visits had been made in 1960, received in 1970 350, 510, and 600 corporate representatives, respectively. Now Willie may not be impressed with these figures, but I must confess that I am. The vigorous recruitment of highly educated blacks by corporations is one of the principal reasons why the proportion of black male workers in white-collar positions increased from 16 to 24 percent from 1964 to 1974 (the proportion of white males in white-collar positions remained slightly over 40 percent during this period) with the greater portion of this increase occurring in the higher level technical, professional, and administrative positions. Indeed, as David Whitman has observed, in the 1960s "the number of blacks in professional and technical positions increased by 131 percent while the number of blacks in managerial and administrative positions increased by 67 percent." Willie, however, chooses to ignore these unprecedented gains for highly trained and educated blacks, preferring instead to emphasize the frustrations of a black violinist in the New York Philharmonic and to belittle my statement that "talented and educated blacks are now entering positions of prestige and influence at a rate comparable to or, in some situations, exceeding that of whites with equivalent qualifications."

However, despite the fact that younger, educated black males have finally reached income parity with younger, educated white males and despite the rapid increase in the number of blacks in higher paying white-collar positions, there is still a significant income gap between all college educated whites and all college educated blacks because of the substantially lower income of older educated blacks. But is this mainly a consequence of present-day discrimination, as Willie wants to believe? No, the comparatively low incomes of older educated blacks is one of the legacies of past discrimination. Denied the opportunity to move into the higher paying occupations when they graduated from college or discouraged from even pursuing such occupational careers, older black college graduates tended to be concentrated in the lower paying fields such as teaching, social welfare, and segregated services; rarely were they employed as managers and professionals in large corporations upon entering the labor market. They therefore, in the words of Freeman, "lack the relevant training or managerial experience to take advantage of new opportunities and advanced only moderately in the new job market." Nonetheless, younger educated blacks are now entering and, indeed, are encouraged to enter, previously neglected fields such as finance, management, chemistry, engineering, accounting, and computer science. Clifton B. Wharton, Jr., Chancellor of the State University of New York, points out, for example, that "in 1966, 45 percent of all black undergraduates were majoring in education; today only 26 percent are. In 1966 only 5 percent of the blacks were studying business, today 18 percent are." For all these reasons and despite modest gains in recent years, the income of older, educated black males lags significantly behind the income of older, educated white males. For all these reasons younger, college educated black males have reached income parity with younger, college educated white males.

COLLEGE EDUCATED BLACK WOMEN

Finally, I should say something about college educated women, another important subgroup hidden in Willie's statistics. College-trained black women, like college-trained white women, have been victimized by sex discrimination over the years. Indeed in the 1970s the major job market problems confronting female black college graduates are associated with sexual and not racial differences. By 1973, for example, although their earnings were significantly below those of both black and white male college graudates, female black college graduates earned nearly $1,000 more than their white counterparts.

BASIC ECONOMIC CHANGES

But I have yet to say anything about less privileged blacks. A comparison of their situation with the unprecedented gains of educated blacks demonstrates, in very sharp relief, the growing class divisions in the black community and the inadequacy of conventional explanations of racial experience. In interpreting my discussion about the improved job situation for more privileged blacks, Willie manages to infer that I "projected these findings upon the poor" because of my statement that "in view of these *developments* (my emphasis) it would be difficult to argue that the plight of the under-class is solely a consequence of racial oppression, that is, the explicit and overt efforts to keep blacks subjugated...." However, the developments to which I refer and which are discussed in several preceding sentences on the same page, are mainly concerned with the creation of a segmented labor market that has grown out of recent structural shifts in our economy—a labor market providing greatly different mobility opportunities for different segments of the black population. This is one of the central arguments of my book, an argument which reflects my concern about the effects of basic economic changes in advanced industrial society, an argument that Willie curiously ignores while he strains to place "the individual mobility" tag on my approach. The consequences of ignoring these structural dimensions in explaining inequality, as far as the black poor are concerned, is one of the subjects to which I now turn.

BLACK UNDER-CLASS

When I argue that "the black experience has moved historically from economic racial oppression experienced by virtually all blacks to economic subordination for the black under-class," Willie complains that I cancel "out racial discrimination as a key cause of poverty among blacks" thereby making it difficult to explain the greater proportion of black families in poverty and the higher unemployment rate for younger blacks. Once again Willie overlooks or chooses to ignore one of my key arguments, namely that "one of the legacies of the racial oppression in previous years is the continued disproportionate black representation in the under-class." In other words, patterns of racial subjugation in the past created a vast black under-class as the accumulation of disadvantages were passed on from generation to generation and the economic and technological revolution of modern industrial society threatens to insure it a permanent status. Accordingly, even if all racial discrimination were eliminated today, the situation of poor blacks will not be substantially improved unless something is done to remove the structural barriers to decent jobs created by changes in our system of production.

Thus, while Willie and some other social scientists continue to stress the problems of race at the expense of emphasizing the problems of economic dislocation under advanced capitalism, class divisions related to greatly different mobility opportunities are growing more rapidly in the black community than in the white community. For example, while young black male college graduates have reached income parity with comparable whites, the income of young black male high school graduates continues to lag behind the income of young white high school graduates. Whereas government antidiscrimination programs, such as affirmative action, have helped to enhance the economic opportunities of trained and educated blacks, such programs have not noticeably improved the economic conditions of poor blacks.

Unlike the life experiences of young privileged blacks, the growing number of black teenagers and young adults, who are isolated in ghettos and are crippled in inferior inner-city schools, do not have the same access to higher paying jobs for which they are qualified as do young whites with similar levels of formal education. Because of the lack of job expansion in the manufacturing sector and the fact that desirable jobs in the service industries require education and training, it matters little whether or not poor blacks graduate from ghetto high schools when they face a situation in which the better paid and more desirable jobs which they can obtain without special skills and/or higher education are decreasing in central cities, not only in relative terms but sometimes in absolute numbers.

In short, because of the historical consequences of racial oppression, under-class blacks find themselves in a situation where they are particularly vulnerable to the negative consequences of uneven economic growth, increasing technology and automation, industry relocation, and labor market segmentation. These are difficult problems that are not going to be addressed by programs based simply upon the premise that current racial discrimination is the major cause of poor blacks' present miseries and limited life chances. Rather these are problems that define the conditions of class subordination, problems that grew out of the previous conditions of racial subordination and are now exacerbated by the economic changes of advanced industrial society. But to repeat, not all blacks are experiencing these difficulties. I would like to make just one more but very important point in this regard — namely, the growing influence of class background on black experiences with both higher and lower education.

CLASS AND BLACK EDUCATION

According to Willie, the opposition from white professionals to minority admission policies in colleges and universities indicates "that talented and educated blacks are not being given access to privilege and power" at a rate comparable to that of whites with equivalent qualifications. Fortunately, this conclusion is not supported by recent data on school enrollment from the U.S. Bureau of the Census. The number of blacks attending colleges and universities in the United States increased from 340,000 in 1966 to 948,000 in 1975. Wharton points out that today the figure has increased to more than a million. Describing the figures on growing black college enrollments as "awesome," he states that "Blacks, who make up 11 percent of America's population, now make up to 10 percent of the 10.6 million college students …. In one year, 1974, the percentage of black high school graduates actually exceeded the percentage of white high school graduates going to college." And, whereas almost half of all black college students were enrolled in predominantly Negro colleges in 1966, today almost 80 percent are attending predominantly white institutions. "These young people constitute the largest concentration of black intellectual manpower in the entire world," states Wharton, "there is now a higher percentage of blacks going to college in America than there is whites going to college in almost every European nation."

It goes without saying that this rapid rise in black college attendance has enormous implications for the further growth of the black middle-class. The class stratification that we observed in the black community today may only be a vague outline of what is to come. This is particularly true when we consider that class or family background for blacks, as shown in the research of the economist Richard B. Freeman and the sociologists Robert Hauser and David Featherman, is becoming an increasingly important factor in determining overall educational attainment and who goes to college. In this connection Freeman points out that "despite all the attention given to enrollment of the ghetto poor into college, it was the children of better educated and wealthier parents who went in increasing numbers in the 1960s." More recent data from the U.S. Department of Commerce reinforce Freeman's conclusion. For example, only 17 percent of both black and white families with incomes of less than $5,000 a year had at least one member (age eighteen to twenty-four) attending college in 1974 and the percentage of family members enrolled in college tended to increase for both blacks and whites as family income increased. Families with incomes of $15,000 had the highest proportion of young adults in college (42 percent for blacks and 50 percent for whites).

But we do not have to restrict ourselves to the examination of the facts on higher education to see the significance of class background in black education and the gap between the haves and the have-nots in the black community. An even more revealing picture emerges when we juxtapose the figures on black higher education with those on black lower education. Specifically, while nearly an equal percentage of white and black high school graduates are entering college, the percentage of young blacks graduating from high school lags significantly behind the percentage of white high school graduates. In 1974, 85 percent of young white adults (twenty to twenty-four years old) but only 72 percent of young black adults graduated from high school. Moreover, only 68 percent of young black adult males graduated from high school. And of those young blacks (eighteen to twenty-four years old) who were not enrolled in college and whose family income was less than $5,000, a startling 46 percent did not graduate from high school (the comparable white figure was 39 percent).

Thus, as the class divisions of the black community grow, it will become increasing difficult for Willie and other social scientists to mask these differences either by speaking of a uniform or single black experience or by presenting gross statistics that neither reflect significant variations in the resources of various subgroups within the black population nor the differences in the effects of race in the past and the effects of race in the present. Andrew Brimmer's warning in 1969 that there is a deepening economic schism in the black community is clearly revealed in the black income, occupational, and educational differences discussed above. And they underscore the central argument of *The Declining Significance of Race* that class has become more important than race in determining black life chances.

WILLIE'S COUNTERHYPOTHESIS

Willie concludes his article by proclaiming that the significance of race is increasing, especially for middle-class blacks who are encountering whites for the first time in integrated situations, for example, in racially integrated neighborhoods. He, therefore, feels that the "people who most experience the pain of dislocation due to the changing times are the racial minorities who are talented and educated and integrated, not those who are impoverished and isolated." After resisting my arguments concerning the growing class differences in the black community, Willie circuitously acknowledges the progress of the talented and educated blacks by discussing the psychological discomforts and pains of dislocation that have accompanied their movement into integrated situations.

Let me say, first of all, that when I speak of the declining significance of race, I am referring to the role it now plays in determining black life chances — in other words, the changing impact of race in the economic sector and, in particular, the importance of race in changing mobility opportunities. Thus, as I have tried to show, as the barriers to entering mainstream occupations were removed for educated blacks, they began to move away from the lower paying professions such as teaching and social work and began in significant numbers to prepare themselves for careers in finance, management, chemistry, engineering, accounting, and other professional areas. Nowhere in my book do I argue that race is "irrelevant or insignificant." It is not simply an either-or situation, rather it is a matter of degree. And I strongly emphasized that there is still a strong basis for racial antagonism on the social, community, and political level.

I do not disagree with the way in which Willie has proposed his counterhypothesis. Many educated blacks do experience psychological discomfort in new integrated situations. Willie and I could probably draw many personal examples of this. We both are black and we both teach at elite universities. A few years ago almost no blacks were in such positions. But I am sure that neither of us would trade places with a poor black trapped in the ghetto and handcuffed to a menial, dead-end, and poorly paid job. That is the real problem in the black community and no cries about the psychological discomfort of the integrated black elite should distract our attention from the abominable and deleterious physical conditions of the isolated black poor.

READINGS SUGGESTED BY THE AUTHOR

Featherman, David L. and Robert M. Hauser. "Changes in the Socio-economic Stratification of the Races, 1962–73." *American Journal of Sociology* 82 (November 1976): 621-49.

Freeman, Richard B. 1976. *Black Elite: The New Market for Highly Educated Black Americans.* New York: McGraw-Hill.

Wharton, Clifton R. Jr. 1978. "Education and Black Americans: Yesterday, Today and Tomorrow." Paper presented at the New York State Black and Puerto Rican Legislative Caucus, Inc., and New York State Conference of Branches, NAACP, February 19.

Whitman, David. 1978. "The Changing Nature of Race Relations Since the Civil Rights Act," Unpublished manuscript. Amherst College, Amherst, M.A.

Wilson, William Julius. 1978. *The Declining Significance of Race: Black and Changing American Institutions.* Chicago: University of Chicago Press.

Chapter 3 ALTERNATIVE PERSPECTIVES ON RACE AND SOCIAL CLASS

During the closing years of the 1970s a major controversy erupted among sociologists in the United States. It had to do with the significance of race in the determination of life chances for blacks. William Wilson declared that race has had less effect than other characteristics on their life chances, particularly in the area of employment. Wilson contended that economic class now is a more important factor than race in determining job placement for blacks and that poverty among inner-city blacks is largely a function of their relatively poor training and inferior schooling [Wilson 1978:110, 120]. I have been a party to this controversy and have debated Wilson in forums at a university and at annual meetings of several professional associations.

I introduced a counterhypothesis that "the significance of race is increasing and that it is increasing especially for middle-class blacks who, because of school desegregation and affirmative action and other integration programs are coming into contact with whites for the first time for extended interaction" [Willie 1979:157].

Wilson also referred to "equal employment legislation" in his discussion of the declining significance of race; in his words, this legislation had "virtually eliminated the tendency of employers to create a split labor market in which black labor is deemed cheaper than white labor regardless of the work performed" [Wilson 1978:110]. Both of us mentioned public law that prohibits discrimination in our arguments. Wilson claimed that such law had created new opportunities for blacks who were sufficiently educated to take advantage of them. Even though disagreeing that the law has been fully effective and that limited education is the prevailing basis for employment discrimination, I, nevertheless, acknowledged that the law had created new desegregated opportunities for blacks and, at the same time, had exposed some who experienced these new opportunities to prejudices that were not present under conditions of segregation. Wilson's hypothesis attempted to explain why the black poor have been left behind. My hypothesis attempted to explain why the black affluent have not yet arrived. When analyzing the effects of antidiscrimination legislation, I emphasized occupation and income disparities between blacks and whites and Wilson emphasized occupation and education disparities within the black population. My analysis was concerned largely with the range of income and occupational opportunities in the present economy. Wilson mainly was concerned with past industrial practices, labor-force trends, and associated behavior [Wilson 1979:159-176; Willie 1979:149-158].

When scholars use different data in their investigations and emphasize different aspects of the same data, there is bound to be disagreement in their conclusions. These differences probably represent different theoretical conceptions of society too. Unfortunately, race-relations research is highly descriptive and tends to proceed without theoretical guidelines explicitly stated. The absence of such is, in part, responsible for the severe controversy that surrounds studies of race, ethnicity, and socioeconomic status. The theoretical concepts that separate the parties to the contemporary controversy on the significance of race for life chances of blacks have been inadequately articulated. Conceptual differences, I believe, are at the root of the controversy.

Wilson's investigation proceeds by defining "three stages of American race relations (the preindustrial, industrial, and modern industrial)." In each of these stages he describes "the role of both the system of production and the state in the development of race and class relations." Wilson contends that, although his book devotes considerable attention to the preindustrial and industrial periods of American race relations, it is his description of the modern industrial period that has generated controversy. He maintains that "in the modern industrial period the economy and the state have, in relatively independent ways, shifted the basis of racial antagonism away from black/white economic contact to social, political, and community issues." The net effect, according to his findings, is that "economic class has been elevated to a position of greater importance than race in determining individual black opportunities for living conditions and personal life experiences" [Wilson 1979:160-61]. Why economic class becomes most important as black-white contact becomes largely social and political is never clearly stated. Wilson concluded that "patterns of racial subjugation in the past created a vast black under-class as the accumulations of disadvantages were passed on from generation to generation and the economic and technological revolution of modern industrial society threatens to insure it a permanent status." No evidence is provided of the extent of intergenerational poverty that is assumed to exist among blacks.

Wilson states that a growing number of black teenagers in ghettos and in the inner city "do not have the same access to higher paying jobs for which they are qualified as do young whites with similar levels of formal education." He attributes inaccessibility of higher paying jobs for blacks not to racial or social discrimination (despite the fact that the blacks are said to be as qualified as the whites who get the jobs) but to "structural barriers to decent jobs created by chance in our system of production" [Wilson 1979:171, 170]. He does not identify discrimination as a contemporary structural barrier in employment.

Wilson does not disagree with the counterhypothesis that I offered about the increasing significance of race, largely because my hypothesis is an attempt to explain the discomfort of some affluent blacks. In Wilson's judgment, however, this is not the real problem in the black community [Wilson 1979:175]. The real problem, as he states it, is "the abominable and deleterious physical conditions of the isolated black poor" [Wilson 1979:175].

Wilson's analysis, which emphasizes historical structural barriers as impediments to human fulfillment, eliminates psychological discomfort and denies social discrimination as a real problem. Wilson's analysis of the human condition of poor blacks ignores some of their fundamental human experiences such as discomfort and discrimination and focuses on physical circumstances as if these were better explanations of their circumstances. Wilson's sociology places humanity at the disposal of history, which, according to Becker, has been a common practice of such scholars as Giddings, Sumner, and even Marx [Becker 1968:78].

HUMANITY AND THE LAW OF HISTORY

Of Marx's analysis, Becker said that Marx had to "shock his age out of its complacency." In his single-minded effort to show that human nature was social and historical and should not be approached psychologically (from within), Marx "threw the whole burden of perfectibility and progress into an automatic law of history." Humanity, in Marx's view, "turned out to be an objective thing, offered up passively to the forces of society and history." Marx was a humanist, said Becker; but he let his humanistic ideas drift to a social and historical determinism. In effect, he sacrificed thinking, feeling, and acting humanity to an ideology [Becker 1968:67, 66].

This is precisely what Wilson also has done in his analysis of the association between race and black life chances. He has sacrificed thinking, feeling, and acting poor blacks to an ideology of historical determinism. Blacks are pictured as passive individuals caught in the tentacles of a process that is beyond their control. Wilson's ultimate goal, of course, is to help poor blacks, even as Marx wished to help the proletariat. But Wilson's world view in the end denies the humanity of those whom he would help.

THE FALLACY OF ECONOMIC DETERMINISM

The ultimate fallacy in Wilson's analysis is similar to the fallacy in Hegel's analysis: "[Hegel] attempts to systematize and to reduce things to monistic principles" [Becker 1968:66]. Although Wilson recognizes such factors as "differential power, racism, [and a] strong sense of group position" as significantly contributing to racial conflict, he believes that such conflict is most aggravated by "intergroup competition for scarce resources" [Wilson 1973:151]. His principal theory is that "racial intolerance tends to be greatest in periods of economic decline, particularly for whites unable to advance themselves and forced by economic strains to compete more heavily with minority groups" [Wilson 1973:150]. Under these conditions, Wilson asserts, "the deteriorating circumstances of many lower-class blacks could worsen" [Wilson 1973:150-51].

Wilson, in his world view of economic determinism in history, discounts the self-initiated efforts of blacks for their own liberation. His assessment is that the nonviolent resistance strategy of blacks proved to be highly effective for only "a brief period of time" [Wilson 1973:131]. He portrays blacks as passive minority participants in a macro-social process that is determined by the white majority. His orientation is illustrated well by this statement: "the moment the dominant group perceives particular minority gains as constituting a distinct threat to its sense of superior position, racial tensions intensify" [Wilson 1973:128]. Essentially, Wilson describes the historical process of group relations as managed by the actions of the dominant people of power, particularly their actions associated with fears and perceptions of threats from others.

I, too, am interested in understanding historical regularities in social relations, particularly in racial and ethnic relations. But I confess that my primary interest is in understanding urgent social problems that affect these populations. I focus less on the past because I know that "whatever regularities one might find ... will be modified by [ongoing] history and by human purpose" [Becker 1968:77]. Ernest Becker said that a sociology that is interested in making the world a better place in which to live "has to observe and analyze the continuing natural social experiments of group living." Thus, he pleaded for "an activist sociology, in addition to an analytic one" [Becker 1968: 76-77].

An activist sociology is cognizant of daily happenings. A criticism I made against Wilson's theory of the declining significance of race was its inconsistency with race-relations reports in the daily newspaper. Indeed, I claimed that "a careful and critical reading of what is currently happening to black and brown populations in this country might have caused William Wilson to be more cautious in his conclusions" [Willie 1981a:28].

SOCIOLOGY AS THE STUDY OF HUMAN EVENTS

My effort has been to study human beings and what they do, by way of sociological analysis. I view sociology as a science of humanity rather than just a science of historical trends. In analyzing the continuing natural experiments of group living, one considers contemporary situations as well as historical trends. Moreover, one studies the psychological and social as well as the physical circumstances of life.

My analysis of contemporary race-relations experiences — those that are antagonistic and those that are harmonious — reveals a range of behaviors and events that contradict the monistic theory of economic determinism advanced by Wilson. In Corpus Christi, Texas, I discovered that the school desegregation court case that aroused much antagonism was financed by a labor union that consisted of black, white and Mexican-American working-class people. These individuals cooperated with each other in a joint effort against discrimination, despite the scarce resources over which they allegedly competed and the segregated neighborhoods in which some lived. But in Indiana, Thomas Pettigrew found that some white workers opposed school desegregation and yet never thought of the interracial neighborhood in which they lived as strange or unusual [Pettigrew 1971: 264].

The Boston mayor said that pairing two working-class communities such as Roxbury, predominantly black, and South Boston, predominantly white of Irish ancestry, would be unacceptable in a school desegregation plan, presumably because of the possibility of violent confrontation between these racial groups that are said to be a threat to each other's economic survival. Yet in Concord, Massachusetts, an affluent, predominantly white, suburb of Boston, there have been fights between Boston-based black students from Roxbury bused to that community daily and local white student residents of the town. These communities and their respective families are not in competition with each other over housing or occupational resources; nevertheless, their students have acted violently against each other.

In some communities, blacks and whites have experienced greater integration in the labor force than they have experienced in residential living. Albert Simkus reports that only recently has the residential integration of affluent blacks with affluent whites begun to catch up with that which has characterized low-income blacks and low-income whites in the past [Simkus 1978: 81–93]. The United States Department of Housing and Urban Development reported that housing discrimination is widespread in the contemporary United States. Specifically, the national audit that the National Committee Against Discrimination In Housing was authorized to conduct discovered that between 20 and 30 percent of all rental or real estate agents contacted discriminated against blacks: agents tended to suggest twice as many apartments or houses for whites who contacted them as for blacks [Eggers 1978:6-8].

With reference to income and occupation discrimination, I obtained these findings in a pilot evaluation study of a leadership-development program for minorities sponsored by the Rockefeller Foundation. My study of black and brown professional and managerial individuals revealed that they received a median annual income that was 15 percentage points less than the median annual income for whites and that educated blacks often had to obtain doctoral degrees to get jobs that were similar to those that some whites obtained with only an undergraduate college education or a master's degree [Willie 1980].

These findings, which come from an examination of contemporary events or "the continuing natural social experiements of group living" (to use Becker's words) are at variance with any monistic theory of interracial antagonism and interracial harmony. As stated by Pettigrew, "the American racial scene has always been highly complex, varied and inconsistent, defying facile generalizations" [Pettigrew 1971:264]. Based on this analysis, I conclude that Wilson's conception of interracial antagonism, as basically a function of economic determinism, is in error. Such a view must be classified as a narrow "detached scientific ... opportunistic inductivism" [Becker 1968:77] that eliminates humanity from the science of human society.

REFERENCES

Becker, Ernest. 1968. *The Structure of Evil.* New York: Free Press.

Dobzhansky, Theodosius. 1951. *Genetics and the Origin of Species.* New York: Columbia University Press.

Eggers, Frederick J., et al. 1978. *Background Information and Initial Findings of the Housing Market Practices Survey.* Washington, D.C.: Department of Housing and Urban Development.

Hyman, Herbert. 1962. *Application of Methods of Evaluation.* Berkeley: University of California Press.

_____, et al. 1955. *Survey Design and Analysis.* New York: Macmillian-Free Press.

Pettigrew, Thomas F. 1971. *Racially Separate or Together.* New York: McGraw-Hill.

Simkus, Albert. 1978. "Residential Segregation by Occupation and Race in Ten Urbanized Areas." *American Sociological Review* 43 (February).

Taylor, Howard F. 1977. "Playing the Dozens with Path Analysis." In R. L. Hall (ed.), *Black Separatism and Social Reality.* New York: Pergamon Press.

Tillich, Paul. 1952. *The Courage to Be.* New Haven: Yale University Press.

U. S. Department of Labor. 1965. *The Negro Family, A Case for National Action.* Washington, D.C.: U.S. Government Printing Office.

Whitehead, Alfred North. 1957. *The Concept of Nature.* Ann Arbor: University of Michigan Press. First published in 1920.

Williams, Robin M., Jr., and Margaret W. Ryan. 1954. *Schools in Transition.* Chapel Hill: University of North Carolina Press.

Willie, Charles V. 1966. "Into The Second Century: Problems of Higher Education of Particular Concern to Morehouse College." *Morehouse College Bulletin* 35 (Spring):7-10.

_____. 1975. *Oreo: A Perspective on Race and Marginal Men and Women.* Wakefield, M.A.: Parameter Press.

_____. 1978. "Racism: Black Education and the Sociology of Knowledge." In C. V. Willie and R. R. Edmonds (eds.), *Black Colleges in America.* New York: Teachers College Press, 3-13.

_____. (ed.). 1979. *The Caste and Class Controversy.* Dix Hills, N.Y.: General Hall.

_____. 1979. "The Inclining Significance Of Race." In C. V. Willie (ed.), *The Caste and Class Controversy.* Dix Hills, N.Y.: General Hall, 145-58.

_____. 1980. *Leadership Development for Minorities: An Evaluation of a Rockefeller Foundation Program.* New York: Rockefeller Foundation.

_____. 1981a. *A New Look at Black Families.* 2d ed. Dix Hills, N.Y.: General Hall.

_____. 1981b. *The Ivory and Ebony Towers.* Lexington, M.A.: Lexington Books of D. C. Heath.

_____. 1981c. "Dominance in the Family: The Black and White Experience." *Journal of Black Psychology* 7 (February): 91–97.

_____. and Susan L. Greenblatt. 1981. "School Desegregation: Racial Politics and Community Conflict Processes." In C. V. Willie and S. L. Greenblatt (eds.), *Community Politics and Educational Change.* New York: Longman, 9–27.

Wilson, William J. 1973. *Power, Racism and Privilege.* New York: Free Press.

_____. 1978. *The Declining Significance of Race.* Chicago: University of Chicago Press.

_____. 1979. "The Declining Significance of Race, Revisited But Not Revised." In Charles V. Willie (ed.), *The Caste and Class Controversy.* Dix Hills, N.Y.: General Hall, 159–76.

PART II

THE CONTINUING SIGNIFICANCE OF RACE IN THE UNITED STATES

Chapter 4   SIGNIFICANCE OF RACE IN THE 1960s

Several years ago, we conducted an ecological investigation of the distribution of a middle-sized city population by age and discovered that a "significant number of adults in all socio-economic areas move at least once in twenty years to a neighborhood of higher status." This finding indicated that a tendency toward upward mobility existed in all segments of the population [Willie 1960:264). There seems to be a natural tendency for families and individual households to improve their circumstances in time.

Yet poverty has not been eliminated in the United States. Why the nation has been unable to eradicate poverty is the issue about which there is much conjecture. Some analysts argue that the upward social mobility described above was largely a function of the motivation, value-orientation, and social organization of immigrant communities which fought their way up as ethnic groups from the bottom of the economic ladder [Glazer 1964]. This same style of reasoning is used to explain why lower-class blacks remain impoverished. The circumstances of many black Americans are frequently explained as a function of the inter-generational transmissions of poverty.

In the United States Department of Labor report *The Negro Family,* Daniel Patrick Moynihan maintained that "a national effort towards the problems of Negro Americans must be directed toward the question of family structure." He looked upon the weakness of the family structure as "the principal source of most of the aberrant, inadequate or anti-social behavior that ... perpetuates the cycle of poverty and deprivation." He concluded that "the present tangle of pathology (among lower-class blacks) is capable of perpetuating itself" (U.S. Depart-

47

ment of Labor 1965: 47, 30). In effect, Moynihan is saying that motivation, value-orientation, and family organization of racial or ethnic group members contribute to the perpetuation or elimination of poverty within that population. The implication is that the family organization and cultural values of blacks differ from those of other ethnic groups and that these account for the persistence of poverty among the members of this racial category. This assertion has been advanced as a basis for social action as if it were supported by empirical evidence. In fact, assertions about the intergenerational transmission of poverty among blacks, such as Moynihan's, are inadequately documented.

TRENDS IN THE PROPORTION OF POOR PEOPLE

The evidence shows that the proportion of the total United States population which is poor today is less than half of the proportion which was poor three or more decades ago. Clearly, some Americans have escaped the poverty which their parents experienced only one generation ago.

Research into the circumstances associated with poverty has not kept pace with the need because too many policymakers have been more interested in justifying the presence or absence of poverty among "their people" rather than explaining it. Thus, the search for solutions to poverty has proceeded within the context of varying ideological orientations.

Moynihan has been identified with the hypothesis that poverty is perpetuated intergenerationally largely because of deficiencies in the family structure. In the United States Department of Labor report, he asserted that "employment ... reflects educational achievement which depends in large part on family stability" (U. S. Department of Labor 1965: 47, 30). This trinitarian association, however, must be understood for what it is—an assertion and not a conclusion based on evidence. In fact, the evidence appears to point in another direction.

Mollie Orshansky raised a serious question about the strength of the association assumed to exist between poverty and family instability when she pointed out that "two-thirds of all children in the families called poor do live in a home with a man at the head" and that "more than half of all poor families report that the head currently has a job." It would seem on the basis of the Orshansky analysis that many poor families are like affluent families. Thus, family instability cannot be considered to be the chief factor associated with poverty among blacks.

A study of income and welfare conducted by the Survey Research Center of the University of Michigan found that characteristics of parents did have a substantial effect on the amount of education their children completed, but that this effect accounted for less than half—41 percent—of the variance in years of school completed [Morgan 1962: 383]. The contribution of a combination of non-family factors to the amount of schooling received by children, therefore, was found to be more important than variables pertaining to the structure and process of the kinship system.

A Census report revealed that "six out of every ten college students in the United States were receiving higher education despite the fact that their fathers did not have this opportunity" (Miller 1964: 26). It is true that youth from higher income families that have college-trained heads are more likely to complete school than poorer youths. Yet it must be stated also that college youth come from all levels of American society. These data mean that no definitive answer is available concerning the extent to which insufficient education received by parents results in limited education and consequently low earning power for their children.

Since family characteristics have some association with the economic status of households, it might be helpful to consider characteristics that could have a significant intergenerational effect. The presence of one or both parents in the household is easily observed and usually is pounced upon as a quick and easy explanation. But, since some low-income families are two-parent households, other variables should be considered. A more subtle but possibly influential variable is the education of the wife and mother in the family. The University of Michigan study discovered that "average education attained by children is also influenced by the educational achievement of the mother. The more education the wife has relative to her husband, the more education the children attain.... Where the wife has less education than the head, achievement of the children is impeded but not so much as they are advanced when the wife has more education than the head" (Morgan 1962: 374–75).

PROMISCUITY, ILLEGITMACY, AND POVERTY

Probably the behavior which has caught the attention of the public more than any other and which is believed to be eminently responsible for the intergenerational transmission of poverty among blacks is illegitimacy. The Department of Labor report authored by Moynihan stated that "the number of illegitimate children per 1,000 life births increased by 11 among whites during a period of two decades but by 68 among nonwhites." The report further stated that of the million or more black illegitimate children in the nation, most of them did not receive public welfare assistance. Nevertheless, illegitimacy was used as one of several indications of family breakdown among blacks which was assumed to be associated with the perpetuation of poverty. Why illegitimacy among whites was not declared to be a circumstance indicative of family breakdown was never clarified. The report stated that "the white family, despite many variants, remains a powerful agency not only for transmitting property from one generation to the next but also for transmitting no less valuable contacts with the world of education and work. White children without fathers, at least, perceive all about them the pattern of men working. Black children without fathers flounder" (U. S. Department of Labor 1965: 8, 12, 34).

Again, a series of assertions have been presented with little evidential base. The implication of these assertions is that part of the source of intergenerational poverty among blacks could be eliminated if illegitimate births could be prevented. In a comparative analysis of problem and stable families in a low-income population, I point out that neither early marriage nor the tendency to marry more than once, nor the tendency to give birth to children out of wedlock causes instability among low-income families. These appear to be effects or consequences of their instability, rather than causes.

The conception of children out of wedlock is often described as a way of life for low-income women, a cultural norm. William Goode believes that many low-income women have few attributes other than sex at their disposal in the process of bargaining for husbands. He arrives at this conclusion based on his study of illegitimacy in the Caribbean Islands (Goode 1960: 28–30). It should go without saying that lower-class women often are exploited by men who have no intention of marrying. But the fact remains that the illegitimate child is frequently a by-product of the woman's search for a husband. Viewed in this perspective, out of wedlock conceptions reflect not so much a breakdown in family structure as a broken promise. The woman submitted as one way of getting her man. All too frequently, he is the man who got away. Thus, sexual activity which may appear to be promiscuous may, in fact, be goal-directed. And a major goal is to induce the suitor to marry and establish a two-parent household. In many cases, the woman misunderstands the paramour and miscalculates with tragic results.

THE CULTURE OF THE POOR

In general, persons who hypothesize that poverty is intergenerationally transmitted due to deficiencies in the person, family, and clan believe that there is a "culture of the poor" (Lewis 1962:2). This concept which may help organize our thoughts about the poor also may tend to inhibit our perceptions of the great variations in behavior among poor people. Their behavior is both similar to and different from the behavior of affluent people in any society. A range of behavior patterns exists among poor people just as a range of behavior patterns exists among the non-poor. Thus, it is inappropriate to look upon the poor as constituting a subculture which reinforces and perpetuates itself, including the condition of poverty. Our studies, which revealed diversified behavior in rent payment practices and in family activities among households in a low-rent public housing project in Syracuse, New York, cast doubt upon the concept of a culture of the poor (Willie, Wagenfield, Cary 1964: 465–70). Of course, there are deficiencies in the life-style of some poor people as there are deficiencies in the life-style of others in the society. But these deficiencies should not be interpreted as an internally consistent, normative, and integrated pattern or as a system of beliefs that guide and give direction to behavior which perpetuates poverty.

POVERTY AND THE SOCIAL SYSTEM

A hypothesis in opposition to the one discussed above is not formulated to explain whether or not poverty is transmitted intergenerationally. However, it does focus upon deficiencies in social systems and in the community at large. This alternative hypothesis is that change in social organization tends to be associated with change in individual behavior. According to this hypothesis, poverty is a function of inadequacies in the operations of social systems; thus, systemic changes are necessary to eliminate poverty among individuals. By implication, then, this hypothesis is relevant to the debate about intergenerational transmission of poverty. The background for this hypothesis is what has happened in this nation, as well as what is known to date about the intergenerational transmission of poverty.

The significant reduction in the proportion of low-income families during the past three decades has occurred largely because of change in the economic system. It has continued to grow and expand, increasing in productivity and efficiency, and has brought more income to people through the years. Thus, much of the poverty that might have been perpetuated intergenerationally was eliminated as a consequence of systemic change — the growth and expansion of the economy.

Certain specific studies of intergenerational poverty also cast doubt on its transmission through families. One, for example, conducted by Lawrence Podell in New York City, discovered that only "15 percent of a citywide sampling of mothers on welfare

rolls ... had parents who also had been relief recipients."
Moreover, Podell found that "eight out of ten believed their
children would not become dependent adults." In the light of
the experience of the mothers included in this study, there is
reason to believe that their predictions might be realized; less
than two out of ten of the current recipients came from families
that received welfare assistance (*New York Times,* March 24,
1968). Failure to receive welfare, however, does not indicate
automatically that 85 percent of the mothers came from non-
poor families. In spite of public concern about increasing welfare
rolls, it is a well-known fact that a large majority of poor
families do not receive needed assistance. Limiting the analysis
to welfare families, however, one finds little evidence to support
the contention that poverty is transmitted intergenerationally.
The evidence indicates that intergenerational transmission is experienced in only a few families.

EDUCATION: PRO AND CON

Many analysts who subscribe to the system-change hypothesis
as a more fruitful approach to an adequate explanation of
poverty believe that the best way to eliminate it is to move in on
the educational system. For instance, a report issued by the Upjohn Institute for Employment Research stated that "the keystone
of any attempt to broaden the employment possibilities for
blacks is obviously education — not only the formal programs of
kindergarten through high school but also education that is now
available in the form of training programs financed by various
federal agencies" (Sheppard and Striner 1966: 22). However,
psychiatrists Abram Kardiner and Lionel Ovesey have not held
much hope for manipulation of the educational system as a way
of dealing with poverty, especially among blacks, unless there is
also a corresponding change in the education of white people.
They state that "the psychosocial expressions of the black personality are the ... end products of the process of oppression.
They can never be eradicated without removing the forces that
create and perpetuate them. What is needed by the black is not

education but re-integration. It is the white ... who requires the education." "There is only one way that the products of oppression can be dissolved," according to Kardiner and Ovesey, "and that is to stop the oppression" (Kardiner and Ovesey 1962: 387). These two psychiatrists consider the inadequate education of blacks—and whatever association may exist between their poverty and education—to be the result of anti-black prejudice and discrimination.

Robert Merton, in his essay, "The Self-Fulfilling Prophecy," supports this view in an illustration of the mechanism at work: whites who prophecy that blacks are incompetent and incapable of benefiting from formal education withhold support from black schools (making them inferior) and then point to the smaller number of black high school or college graduates (which the inferior schools produce) as justification for not providing greater support for the education of blacks (Merton 1949: 179-95). In his commentary on schools in metropolitan areas, James B. Conant observed that "we now recognize so plainly but so belatedly [that] a caste system finds its clearest manifestation in an educational system" (Conant 1961: 11–12).

If the educational system in this country is to change so that it serves the needs of black people better, those people who established and continue to maintain a system of inferior education for blacks must change. They must support an educational system which equips blacks with the skills to participate productively in the mainstream of a technology-dominated economy. This, however, is not likely to occur unless whites are reoriented in their education and general socialization to relate to blacks as human beings, divested of any belief that whites are superhuman. Kardiner and Ovesey point out that blacks were subjected to pure utilitarian use during the period of slavery in this country. "Once you degrade someone in that way," they remind us, "the sense of guilt makes it imperative to degrade the object further to justify the entire procedure." (Kardiner and Ovesey 1962: 379). Merton doubts the efficacy of education as a way of dealing with the prevailing patterns of race relations. His belief is that "education may serve as an operational adjunct but not as the chief basis for any but excruciating slow change in the prevailing patterns of race relations" (Merton 1949: 183). What is likely to be more effective, according to Merton, is "deliberate institutional change" designed to destroy discrimination (Merton 1949: 193).

RACIAL DISCRIMINATION AND POVERTY

Economist Herman Miller, who also subscribes to the hypothesis of institutional change as a way of dealing with poverty among disadvantaged minority groups, maintains that "racial discrimination is a key cause" of the black's perpetually low estate. He refers to a study of the Council of Economic Advisers which estimated that, during a single year, $13 billion more would have been placed in the hands of blacks had there not been any racial discrimination in employment (Miller 1965: 32 in B. B. Seligman). He points out that black people with the same amount of education as whites usually earn less money. In an analysis of the Census, Miller discovered that "non-white men earn about three-fourths as much as whites with the same amount of schooling," and that "blacks who have completed four years of college education can expect to earn only as much in a lifetime as whites who have not gone beyond the eighth grade." Thus, Miller concludes, "there is some justification for the feeling by Puerto Ricans, blacks and other minority groups that education does not do as much for them, financially, as it does for others" (Miller 1964: 140-153).

It would appear that racial and ethnic discrimination, more than inadequate education, is one of the chief factors contributing to the low-income status of many blacks. For example, among whites of limited education (with eight or fewer years of schooling), 50 percent are likely to have jobs as service workers or laborers at the bottom of the heap, while nearly 80 percent of black workers with limited education are likely to find work only in these kinds of jobs (Miller 1964: 140–53).

That racial discrimination is one of the major factors contributing to economic deprivation among blacks is illustrated by an interview which one of the field workers in Hylan Lewis'

Child Rearing Study conducted with a fifty-year-old white painter who was also a foreman for a construction company. A part of the interview record, arranged in dialogue form, follows:

Interviewer:	Do you have any blacks working under you?
Foreman:	No. Right now we are building a house for an Army colonel. We never use blacks in jobs in the suburban area because that would hurt the company's reputation.
Interviewer:	Do you ever use blacks?
Foreman:	When we have a job in Washington we hire a large number of blacks.
Interviewer:	Why?
Foreman:	The black painter is able and willing to do the same job for only half the pay of a white painter. Give me a crew of six niggers and we'll knock out a five-story office building in a week. They all got families and half-pay is damn good money for a nigger. (Jackson 1966: 29).

James Tobin has pointed out that the low earning capacity of blacks and their inferior education "both reflect discrimination" (Tobin 1965: 746–47). The point we continue to emphasize, however, is that even when work capacity and education are equal to those of whites, discrimination still persists and results in a lower family income for blacks. The Moynihan thesis that the lack of improvement in opportunities for a large mass of black workers is correlated with a serious weakening of the black family, therefore, obscures the issue of discrimination and white racism in America and so does his statement that "equality, as a fundamental democratic disposition goes beyond equal opportunity to the issue of equal results." (Moynihan 1965.) The Census data analyzed by Miller indicated that equal opportunity has not yet been realized for black Americans; thus discussion of equal results is indeed premature.

We know that the rise in income in the past twenty to thirty years has been shared by black and white families and that the percent of black and white families below the poverty line has been significantly reduced, according to the Bureau of Labor Statistics (Bureau of Labor Statistics 1967: 18). The two populations, however, started from a different base. Sixty-five percent of black families were poor two to three decades ago, compared with only 27 percent of white families. In 1974, the proportions had changed radically, but the relative incomes of the two racial populations remained the same. Thus, 23 percent of blacks received family incomes under $4,000 during the mid-1970s; only 7 percent of whites received income at this low level. The proportion of blacks in poverty was two to three times greater than the proportion of poor whites two to three decades ago, and this ratio has remained constant over the years.

DIFFERENT APPROACHES FOR ELIMINATING POVERTY AMONG WHITES AND BLACKS

Because there are twice as many poor blacks proportionately as there are poor whites and because racial discrimination has been identified as a key cause which keeps blacks at the bottom (an experience which they do not share with poor whites), it could very well be that different hypotheses are needed for explaining the continuation of poverty in the two racial populations. Failure to explore the possibility that different explanations of poverty may be required for different racial populations, which have had essentially different experiences, may have contributed to the contemporary controversy. It is conceivable, for example, that the hypothesis which may contribute to a better understanding of poverty among whites is one which seeks to determine the association, if any, between low-income status, on one hand, and motivation, aspiration, life-orientation, and the presence or absence of primary group supports, on the other. For blacks, however, a more powerful explanation of poverty might proceed from an examination of the hypothesis which seeks to determine the association, if any, between low-income status and discrimination, oppression, injustice, and the institutional controls that govern these phenomena.

The findings of another study, which we conducted in Washington, D.C., are the basis for suggesting the possibility of differential explanations of poverty in white and black populations. The study dealt with juvenile delinquency among whites and blacks. We discovered that reducing family instability would probably contribute to a greater reduction in delinquency among whites than among blacks and that increasing economic opportunities would very likely contribute to a greater reduction in delinquency among blacks than whites. While a good deal of family instability existed with the black population in Washington, economic insecurity was overwhelming. It appeared, according to the data collected, that we could not get at the family instability factor and its association with delinquency without first dealing with economic insecurity and its association with delinquency. Because a higher proportion of whites were not poor, family instability was their outstanding problem. But economic insecurity was the salient problem for blacks and it could not be circumvented in favor of family instability (Willie 1967: 326–35).

The same principle may apply to the issue of poverty. Institutional changes during the past three to four decades have resulted in a substantial reduction in the proportion of whites who are poor. External changes in social organization have upgraded most of the white population beyond the poverty level. The few who remain poor probably have problems which are more personal and less susceptible to mass amelioration through institutional manipulation. These whites may be the individuals with insufficient motivation, low aspiration, and a fatalistic orientation unreached thus far by changes in the institutional systems of society which create new opportunities. The proportion of poor blacks, however, remains at a higher level and may still be amenable to ameliorative mass efforts. Apparently, the kinds of institutional changes needed to upgrade the black population are somewhat different from those required to upgrade the white population. In addition to deliberate institutional changes which may increase economic opportunities, blacks require deliberate institutional changes which will prevent racial discrimination. Until these are put into effect, we cannot know how large the residual proportion of black poor people might be who need such individualized attention as the few poor whites may now require. To date, three-fourths of the black population have been upgraded beyond poverty. There is every reason to believe that more can and must be done.

PROBLEM WITH MOYNIHAN PROPOSAL

In the light of this discussion, it would seem that one problem with the Moynihan proposal for dealing with poverty is that it projects a solution more appropriate for the white than for the black poor. Projecting has been going on for a long time. Whites tend to project upon blacks solutions to social problems that are of value for whites, without understanding that experiences and conditions for blacks may be different. One essential difference with reference to poverty is that blacks also experience a great deal of discrimination and that the institutional changes which helped pull more than nine out of every ten whites above the poverty line have not run their full course for blacks, especially those institutional changes and social controls which prohibit discrimination. This is why the Moynihan concern about equal results is premature until there are equal opportunities.

CONCLUSIONS

On the basis of the foregoing analysis, we conclude the following:

1. There is some intergenerational transmission of poverty, though not as much as is generally assumed.
2. Upward social mobility is a more common experience in the United States than the continuation of intergenerational poverty.

3. The perpetuation of poverty from one generation to the next is likely to be a function of personal and family-connected circumstances as well as patterns of institutional organization.

4. Personal and family-connected circumstances are likely to be more powerful explanations of poverty among whites than among blacks.

5. Institutional arrangements and patterns of social organization are likely to be more powerful explanations of the presence of poverty among black than among white people in the United States.

The latter two conclusions are stated tentatively and should be further tested as hypotheses. The reason for suggesting a differential explanation for the continuation of poverty by race is the fact that whites and blacks have dissimilar patterns of participation in the economic system of the United States. As stated by Louis Kriesberg in "Intergenerational Patterns of Poverty," "generational change in the proportion of the population which is poor is largely determined by economic developments and public policies regarding income maintenance and distribution" (Kriesberg, 1968: 5–6). Racial discrimination has prevented blacks and other non-white minorities from participating fully in the benefits of an expanding economy. Even the income maintenance programs available to minorities have been encumbered with punitive restrictions so that their full value has not been experienced. Changes in institutional arrangements have been largely responsible for preventing poverty among whites and there is reason to believe that such changes will aid in the prevention of poverty among blacks if the benefits of these changes are made available to all sectors of society.

Because whites, in general, have had free access to the opportunities produced by institutional change, the residual number of poor people in this racial category might well be a function of personal and family-connected deficiencies. It is not concluded that poverty among whites cannot be further reduced by more changes in the institutional systems of society. Rather, it is suggested that new manipulations of social institutions will probably net a smaller rate of change in the proportion of poor whites, since most whites who could benefit from these major institutional changes have already taken advantage of them.

REFERENCES

Bureau of Labor Statistics and U.S. Bureau of the Census. *Social and Economic Conditions of Negroes in the United States* (Washington: U.S. Government Printing Office, October 1967, BLS Report No. 332, Current Population Reports, Series P-23, No. 24), p. 18.

Conant, James B. *Slums and Suburbs* (New York: McGraw-Hill Book Co., 1961), pp. 11-12.

Goode, William J. "Illegitimacy in the Caribbean Social Structure," *American Sociological Review,* 25 (February, 1960), pp. 20-30.

Glazer, Nathan and Moynihan, Daniel Patrick. *Beyond the Melting Pot* (Cambridge: The M.I.T. Press and Harvard University Press, 1964).

Jackson, Luther P., (ed.) *Poverty's Children (The Child Rearing Study of Low Income Families in the District of Columbia)* (Washington: Health and Welfare Council of National Capital Area, 1966), p. 29.

Kardiner, Abram and Ovesey, Lionel. *The Mark of Oppression* (Cleveland: Meridian Books, 1962), p. 387.

Kriesberg, "Inter-Generational Patterns Of Poverty," (paper presented at the annual meeting of the Eastern Sociological Society, Boston, Mass., April 6, 1968), pp. 5-6.

Lewis, Oscar. *Five Families* (New York: Science Editions, 1962), p. 2.

Merton, Robert K., *Social Structure and Social Theory* (New York: The Free Press, 1949), pp. 179-195.

Miller, H. *Rich Man, Poor Man* (New York: Thomas Y. Crowell Co., 1964), p. 26.

Miller, H. "The Dimensions of Poverty," Ben B. Seligman (ed.) *Poverty as a Public Issue* (New York: Free Press, 1965), p. 32.

Morgan, N., et al. *Income and Welfare in the United States* (New York: McGraw-Hill Book Co., 1962) p. 383.

Moynihan, Daniel P., "Employment, Income and the Ordeal of the Negro Family," *Daedalus,* 94 (Fall 1965).

The New York Times "Survey of Relief Shows Tie to Past," March 24, 1968.

Orshansky, Mollie. "Consumption, Work and Poverty," Ben B. Seligman (ed.) *Poverty as a Public Issue* (New York. The Free Press, 1965), pp. 55-56.

Sheppard, Harold L. and Striner, Herbert E. *Civil Rights Employment and the Social Status of American Negroes* (Kalamazoo: The W. E. Upjohn Institute for Employment Research, 1966), p.22.

Tobin, James. "On Improving the Economic Status of the Negro," *Daedalus,* 94 (Fall 1965), pp. 746-747.

United States Department of Labor. *The Negro Family. A Case for National Action* (Washington: U.S. Government Printing Office, March 1965), pp. 47, 30.

Willie, Charles V., "Age Status and Residential Stratification," *American Sociological Review,* 25 (April 1969), p. 264.

Willie, Charles V., "Family Status and Economic Status in Juvenile Delinquency," *Social Problems,* 14 (Winter 1967), pp. 326-335.

Willie, Charles V., Wagenfeld, Morton O. and Cary, Lee J., "Patterns of Rent Payment Among Problem Families," *Social Casework,* 45 (October, 1964), pp. 465-470.

Chapter 5 SIGNIFICANCE OF RACE IN THE 1970s

When the popular press was lavishing attention upon Wilson's work and the professional journals were providing extensive space for commentaries, other important studies about race relations in the United States in the 1970s received only limited attention. Such was the study prepared by Dorothy Newman and colleagues entitled, *Protest, Politics and Prosperity* and subtitled *"Black Americans and White Institutions, 1940–75."*

Richard Margolis, in *Change* magazine, states that "in the war of reviews Wilson has won hands down ... even the *New York Times,* not the world's most roseate journal, considers Wilson's sophisticated optimism more convincing than Newman's straightforward gloom" (Margolis 1979:106).

This discussion of the continuing significance of race begins with a statement of social practice reported in newspapers rather than with a series of propositions derived from sociology studies. There is no suggestion in this approach that the methods of journalism and sociology are the same. Yet sociologists ought to seriously take into consideration what is happening around them in the formulation of their principles and propositions. A careful and critical reading of what is currently happening to black and brown populations in this country might have caused William Wilson to be more cautious in his conclusions.

Race relations is a continuous reminder in the United States of the requirements of the Constitution. It is one of the best indicators of how near this nation has come and how far it has failed to fulfill the basic commitment of justice for all. If this thesis is correct, then race relations in the United States is a prime indicator of the viability of this society as a democracy.

63

Rather than declining in significance, race, as such an indicator, is of continuing significance.

This does not mean that, psychologically, there are not attempts to repress race as an indicator of the strength or weakness of our social system. The optimistic statements about the achievement of racial minorities in the United States, that are readily accepted and uncritically adopted by the majority or the dominant people of power, is, in effect, an attempt to repress our failures in race relations. Optimistic assessments are used as antidotes against feelings of guilt regarding our failures.

Repression prevents the development of guilt that could mobilize the nation to do better. In race relations, denial is a common way of dealing with guilt. It has been said that "a guilty conscience is the seasoning of our daily life" (Tournier 1962:10). Guilt is so difficult to deal with once it is acknowledged that the dominant people of power often attempt to put into the minds of the weak the guilt that is their own (Tournier 1962:14).

Failure to fulfill the requirements of our common codes such as those contained in the Constitution is certainly a basis for guilt. Race relations is one area in which our failure is clearly manifested. Therefore, race relations in the United States is the source of much guilt for the majority. When the burden of guilt is great, the circumstances that contribute to the guilt must be changed or else the guilt has to be denied. Thus, optimistic assessments of race relations are welcome relief for those who are carrying a heavy burden of guilt.

A recent editorial in the *Dallas Morning News* attests to the fact that racism or racist behavior has the potential to evoke much guilt among members of the majority. The techniques used by the editors of that paper to reduce the guilt were denial and a proposal for suppression. They deny that outright racial hatred exists now except perhaps among "Klansmen and unrepentant Black Panthers" and declare that racism really was a phenomenon of the 1930s when Nazis hated Jews and maybe of the 1960s during the civil rights movement in this country. Specifically, the *Dallas Morning News* editorial states that "there are few racists in the full-blown 1930s or even 1960s sense. But there are many Americans who every day are smeared all over with the imputation of racial hostility just because they differ with self-anointed spokesmen for other races." The newspaper implied that the smear was unfair and that the terms of racism or racist abused those whose behavior was so classified. Having declared that "it would be hard, in point of fact, to prove that in the United States anything like outright racial hatred persists" (this is the technique of denial), the *Dallas Morning News* concluded that the terms racism and racist are stale and weary and should be retired from our language (this is the technique of suppression).

The newspaper editorial acknowledged that there may be members of the white majority who are insensitive to racial minority aspirations, who support reduced federal spending programs that benefit minorities, or who believe that there is nothing wrong with the intelligence tests because minorities may score lower on them than do whites. However, the paper believes that to hate a person because of his or her race is "a bad thing" but to deny a person "this or that favor" is something else and should not be classified as racism or racist behavior. The alleged negative behavior of some whites toward blacks, in the opinion of the *Dallas Morning News,* should be labeled by another word other than racism or racist (*Dallas Morning News,* September 23, 1979).

While the editors of a major newspaper in Dallas were declaring that the terms racism and racist now "cease to mean anything in particular," black women in the same city were bringing a suit against the prestigious Republican National Bank of Dallas charging discrimination. Even before the *Dallas Morning News* editorial was written, Judge Patrick Higginbotham of the federal district court in Dallas ruled that "the plaintiffs have demonstrated, at least, prima facie evidence that [the Republican National Bank's] personnel practices have been infested to the core by racial and sex discrimination." For example, blacks in 1969 constituted 7.56 percent of the bank's work force but only 0.34 percent of its managers. "What makes this case so complicated," said one of the attorneys representing the plaintiffs, "is that it involves white-collar workers." The particular charges against this giant banking industry in a city where "outright racial hatred" does not persist, according to its morning newspaper, are interesting. One black woman, a college graduate, claims that she was not accepted in the bank's management trainee program to which she had applied; and another black woman alleged that she was dismissed as a clerical employee because she had married a white man. The *New York Times* reports that "the bank has prepared a massive amount of documentation to contest the charges and plans to call on its personnel officers, labor market analysts, sociologists, and statistical experts to back up its contention that it has not been remiss in its hiring and promotion of qualified blacks and women" (*New York Times,* November 5, 1979).

This case is clinical evidence that race continues to be significant as the alleged basis for denying opportunities to people who are not white. Moreover, the opportunities allegedly denied are in the private economic sector at the managerial and clerical level, where the applicants are not individuals with limited education.

In the governmental sector, where we have been told that talented minorities also are getting good jobs at an unprecedented rate (Wilson 1978), it is interesting to note the continuing effect of race. The election of Richard Arrington, Jr. as mayor of Birmingham, Alabama in 1979 was hailed as proof that that city had made significant racial progress. Arrington, who is black, defeated Frank Parsons, a white lawyer. But Arrington's victory was due to voting that was sharply divided along racial lines. According to the *Boston Globe,* "45 percent of the voters of Birmingham are black and 77 percent of them voted, almost all of them for Arrington. Only 66 percent of the white voters turned out and [only] 10 percent of them also voted for Arrington. Arrington took 52 percent of the vote" (*Boston Globe,* November 2, 1979).

An editorial in the *Boston Globe,* hailing the election of a black mayor, cautioned that the public should not be "misled into thinking that Birmingham is a city where there is no racism." Indeed, Arrington's decision to seek election was due to the refusal of the incumbent mayor to fire a white police officer who had shot and killed an unarmed black woman. And, as stated earlier, the voting was sharply divided along racial lines, with a majority of white voters casting their ballots for the white candidate and a majority of blacks voting for the black candidate (*Boston Globe,* November 2, 1979).

Even though an editorial in the *Boston Globe* attributes the nonviolent way that executive authority in city government in Birmingham was transferred from whites to blacks as resulting from "white and black moderates working together," the facts reveal that only 10 percent of the whites voted for the first black mayor of that city; 90 percent preferred the white candidate (*Boston Globe,* November 2, 1979). This fact means that power tends to concede authority only when forced to do so. Thus whites in the United States tend to transfer political authority to black and brown populations only when their own numbers dwindle, when those of opposing groups increase, or when they lose control over coercive institutions such as the police department and the court. Birmingham elected its first black mayor only after blacks had increased to 45 percent of the voting population.

Lee Sloan and Robert French, who prepared a case study entitled "Black Rule in the Urban South?" state that "holding the line against black power seems to be a growing problem for metropolitan white America." They state that "it is becoming increasingly evident that whites moving out may be forfeiting political control to the blacks who are left behind." Whites attempt to regain control, according to Sloan and French, by "redefining political boundaries so that the proportion of blacks within the new political unit is decreased drastically." They say that this method of regaining control "can assume the forms of gerrymandering or annexation." Also, they classify the at-large election as another way of retaining control as numbers of a majority population began to dwindle (Sloan and French 1977:200).

Certainly the Houston experience is an illustration of the function of at-large elections in race relations in maintaining control by the dominants. The *New York Times* reported that "during Houston's quarter-century rise to national stature as the country's fifth largest city, its spectacular expansion has essentially been managed — or mismanaged, say a growing army of critics—by a network of businessmen and developers ... dissenters have had little voice in all this, least of all the blacks and Mexican Americans." As a result of pressure from the U.S. Justice Department, the city has agreed to a new voting arrangement by districts and at-large that will put minority representatives on the city council and, thereby, alter its governmental power structure. The *New York Times* states that "under the old system, all members of the Council were elected at large, which diluted the voting strength of blacks and Mexican Americans." Under the old system, "the minorities, who make up 40 to 45 percent of the city's population, have had only one representative on the city council." Under the new arrangement, five of the fourteen council members are elected at-large and the others are chosen from each of nine geographical districts. The election by single-member districts guarantees that three or four black or Hispanic candidates are elected (*New York Times,* November 1, 1979).

The Justice Department moved against the at-large election system of Houston and other big cities in Texas on the basis of authority granted to it under amendments of the Voting Rights Act of 1965 to review certain local election systems.

The past decisions of whites to move from city to suburban communities have strengthened the capacity of black and of brown populations to control city governments. Were these populations not contained within the city because of housing discrimination, their numbers would not be large enough to wrest control from whites. Thus, housing discrimination, which has contributed to racial concentration, has strenghthened the capacity of racial minorities to influence the public policies of cities in this nation.

On the basis of press reports, we know that inadequate education is not the basis for discrimination against black and brown populations in the United States, that racism is at the core of the rejection process. Let us take police departments and the courts as examples. Boston, Cincinnati, and New York are under court order to increase the number of minorities. High-level educational attainment is not required of police. In all cities mentioned, a charge of racial discrimination in the recruitment and promotion of police officers was made. Of the 269 sergeants on the Boston police force in July 1980, one was black and two other blacks with permanent sergeant ratings served in higher non-civil service posts. Moreover, there were no black lieutenants or captains. About 5 percent of the force in 1980 was black according to a consent decree filed in the federal district court (*Boston Globe,* July 10, 1980).

Cincinnati has a police force that consisted of only a few blacks and was charged with violating the Civil Rights Act of 1964 and other federal statutes. The Justice Department charged that the police department of Cincinnati "had failed or refused to recruit, hire, promote and assign blacks and women on the same basis as white men and had used written tests that excluded blacks and women. Cincinnati, in a consent decree filed in a federal district court, promised to fill one-third of the police officer vacancies with blacks and one-fourth of the openings for specialists and sergeants with blacks and women in terms of their numbers on the 1980 police recruitment list or in the pool of eligible employees," according to The *New York Times* (July 9, 1980).

The Executive Director of the New York Civil Liberties Union states that "the New York City Police Department ... [in 1980] has one of the lowest percentages of minority officers of any major city.... At issue is a test which, in effect, screens out members of minority groups but which has never been shown to be an accurate predictor of an applicant's job performance." The city would not sign a consent decree as an indication of its commitment to the goal of equal opportunity and had to be forced by a court order of the United States Court of Appeals to hire one minority police officer for every two white officers hired (*New York Times,* July 15, 1980). The initial response of the mayor of New York City to the court order was to postpone hiring, pending the outcome of a legal appeal. The mayor also criticized another court ruling that sanctioned as lawful a federal public works program that reserves 10 percent of such projects for minority contractors. At first, he declared that he would not "give in" to the court order regarding police hiring.

Finally, the courts, which have been the principal means through which racial minorities and women have secured constitutional rights, have been found wanting in their own employment practices. According to one press bulletin, "data supplied ... by federal courts confirm accusations that, for the most part, the courts provide only lowly jobs for women and members of minorities." Representative Don Edwards states that information compiled for the House of Representatives Subcommittee on Civil and Constitutional Rights shows "that with few exceptions employment practices in the federal judiciary have excluded minorities and women in all but clerical and secretarial positions." According to United Press International, Federal District Court Judge Elmo B. Hunter of Missouri, testifying on behalf of the Judicial Conference of the United States, acknowledged that the allegations were "more accurate than inaccurate" (*New York Times,* June 1, 1980).

With the courts exhibiting ambivalence in acknowledging their full guilt with reference to minority hiring, one can understand how this nation has been flooded with a series of crazy, mixed-up, court-ordered school desegregation plans that have tended to grant more desegregation relief to whites, who, in most instances, were against desegregation and have left most blacks, the plaintiffs, who won the cases seeking desegregation relief, in segregated, racially isolated schools. The school desegregation plan initially ordered by a federal district court in Dallas left two-thirds of the black students in segregated, racially isolated schools; and the plan initially ordered by a federal district court in St. Louis left three-fourths of the black students in segregated, racially isolated schools. In both cities more whites than blacks experienced the benefits of school desegregation, according to the court-ordered plans. The reason for this bizarre turn of events was the assumption, sometimes implicit, sometimes explicit, on which the plans were based — that whites ought always to be the majority in desegregated schools that provide a quality education. In instances where whites were only half or less than half of the schoolwide population, too few were available to desegregate predominantly black schools if whites always had to be the majority. Whether or not there is an association between some of the inappropriate assumptions on which some court-ordered school desegregation plans are based and the minuscule number of racial minority persons employed by federal courts in professional capacities is worthy of investigation.

Up to this point, a number of cases or illustrations have been provided. The weight of evidence certainly would cause one to question a proposition that asserts that race is declining in significance. But clinical evidence does not command the respect of more systematically gathered data that uses the methodologies of the social sciences.

Based on a sample of 15,170 in a large nondecennial survey conducted in 1976, the U.S. Civil Rights Commission found that when all things were equal, including age, sex, occupation, and other characteristics, black and other minority males received an annual income that was 15 to 20 percentage points less than that received by white men (Civil Rights Commission 1978:53-54). There is no ethical or just reason why black people should receive 15 to 20 percentage points less income than whites. I call this income discrepancy an unfair tax that qualified minorities pay for not being white. It is a racist tax that is withheld from their annual earnings and, consequently, is a form of institutional racism. In an evaluation study commissioned by the Rockefeller Foundation that involved a small sample of blacks and whites in all geographic regions who were matched by age, sex, and broad occupational categories at professional and managerial levels, I obtained a result that was similar to the finding of the Civil Rights Commission. The black and brown professional and managerial individuals in my small sample study received a median annual income that was 15 percentage points less than the median annual income for whites (Willie 1980). Indeed, I found that educated blacks had to obtain doctoral degrees to get jobs that were similar to those that some whites obtained with only a college education or a master's degree. But even after occupational parity had been achieved because of their extraordinary education, blacks lagged behind whites with similar jobs in the income they received.

The report *All Our Children* by the Carnegie Council presents data by race and income analyzed by Rhona Pavis, who found that "90 percent of the income gap between blacks and whites is the result ... of lower pay for blacks with comparable levels of education and experience" (Keniston 1977:92).

I do not know the basis for this conclusion and decided to make some calculations of my own based on data presented in the Current Population Reports (U.S. Census Bureau 1978). My goal was to determine how much of the total income difference between whites and blacks or other minorities was due to the presence of racial discrimination and the absence of effective affirmative action practices to overcome such discrimination.

By keeping the analysis at the macro-social level and by determining what had happened to the total population of black and other minorities of the race parameter, I obtained these results based on the assumptions that (1) black and other minority household heads should be randomly distributed throughout all occupations so that their percentage in any particular category is the same as their percentage in the total population of the employed; (2) the median annual income is a representative figure for each household; and (3) blacks and other racial minorities ought to receive the same median income that whites receive.

On the basis of these assumptions, my calculations revealed (in Table 1) that the 4.1 million households that were headed by blacks who were employed for some period of time in 1976 should have received $67.3 billion in annual income rather than $49.7 billion. In 1976, according to my calculations, racial discrimination cost employed blacks and other racial minorities $17.6 billion.

One reason blacks were $17.6 billion down from what they should have received, as shown in Table 1c, is because affirmative action had not overcome the selective employment practices by race that characterizes American society. In the high-paying professional, managerial, sales, and skilled-craft jobs, there were only 1.1 million racial minorities when there should have been 2.3 million if there had been equity in employment.

TABLE 1

Number and Income of Black and of White Workers for
Longest Job Held by Household Head, U.S.A., 1976

Table 1a

	Number		Median Income	
Occupation	Black	White	Black	White
Professional, Technical, and Kindred Workers	345	6,191	$17,286	$21,925
Managers and Administrators	218	6,677	17,397	21,550
Sales Workers	86	2,557	13,706	18,681
Clerical and Kindred Workers	452	3,160	11,079	15,470
Craft and Kindred Workers	484	8,682	15,211	17,302
Operatives	1,075	6,837	13,164	14,688
Laborers	389	1,679	11,413	13,208
Farm Workers	126	1,609	4,765	12,685
Service Workers	881	2,929	8,284	12,374
Total or Median	4,056	20,321	$12,199	$17,228

Table 1b

	Number of Blacks		
Occupation	Without Affirmative Action	With Affirmative Action	Difference
Profesional, Technical, and Kindred Workers	345	588	+ 243
Managers and Administrators	218	621	+ 403
Sales Workers	86	238	+ 152
Clerical and Kindred Workers	452	325	− 127
Craft and Kindred Workers	484	825	+ 341
Operatives	1,075	712	− 363
Laborers	389	186	− 203
Farm Workers	126	156	+ 30
Service Workers	881	343	− 538

TABLE 1 (cont.)

Table 1c

Occupation	Total Income of Blacks			
	(a) Inequitable Number and Median[a]	(b) Inequitable Number but Equitable Median[b]	(c) Equitable Number and Equitable Median[c]	(a)/(c) Difference[d]
Professional and Technical Workers	$ 5,963,670,000	$ 7,564,125,000	$12,891,900,000	−$6,928,230,000
Managers and Administrators	3,792,546,000	4,697,900,000	13,382,550,000	− 9,590,004,000
Sales Workers	1,178,716,000	1,606,566,000	4,446,078,000	− 3,267,362,000
Clerical and Kindred Workers	5,007,708,000	6,993,344,000	5,028,400,000	− 20,692,000
Craft and Kindred Workers	7,362,124,000	8,374,168,000	14,274,150,000	− 6,912,026,000
Operatives	14,151,300,000	15,789,600,000	10,457,856,000	+ 3,693,444,000
Laborers	4,439,657,000	5,137,912,000	2,456,688,000	+ 1,982,969,000
Farm Workers	600,390,000	1,598,310,000	197,808,000	+ 402,582,000
Service Workers	7,298,204,000	10,901,494,000	4,244,282,000	+ 3,053,922,000
Total	$49,794,315,000	$62,663,419,000	$67,379,712,000	− $17,585,397,000

a. Existing number of black workers X median income of blacks in occupational group.

b. Existing number of black workers X median income of whites in occupational group.

c. Number of black workers in occupational group is the same as proportion in total labor force nationwide and median income is the same as that for whites in occupational group.

d. The income that black workers would receive under condition of equity or effective affirmative action.

Source of data for Table 1a: Bureau of the Census, *Money Income in 1976 of Family and Persons in the United States* (Current Population Reports, Series P-60, No. 114), Washington, D.C.: U.S. Government Printing Office, 1978, pp. 143, 145.

These high-paying jobs in a free and open and equitable society would have contributed two-thirds of the total income received by the population of blacks and other minorities if there had been as many racial minorities as there should have been in these jobs; those who managed to get employment in them were paid on the average one-fifth less than whites who held similar positions. Thus, these four high-paying occupational categories accounted for only one-third of the total income for blacks and other racial-minority households, because of the limitations imposed by racial discrimination.

Unlike the white population, in which two-thirds of the income for the group came from these higher-paying jobs, the black population received two-thirds of its income from the lower status occupations. It is fair to say, on the basis of these findings, that the black community continues to be supported largely by the wealth of its blue-collar workers.

Despite the increase in education of blacks, the data revealed that only 3 percent of the managers and administrators came from black or other minority household heads in 1976; that there were two-thirds fewer than there should have been; and that, collectively, they earned $9.5 billion less than they would have earned had there not been any discrimination in the number of minorities employed in these occupations and in the salaries that they received. This occupational category showed the highest discrepancy between what was and should have been; it was followed by professional and technical workers, for whom the discrepancy was down $6.9 billion from what it should have been. The depressed income of the white-collar and skilled workers contributed more significantly to the $17.6 billion income deficit that black and other minorities experienced because of discrimination than did wages received or the over-representation in numbers of minorities in blue-collar occupations.

Because $17.6 billion in 1976 would have come to black and other minorities had they not been discriminated against, I conclude that race is significantly associated with these outcomes and continues to influence the income and occupational life chances of the racial minorities and of the majority in this nation, including the affluent as well as the poorer sectors of their populations and that the economic effect of racial discrimination for blacks is greater among the affluent than among the poor.

With reference to poor blacks and poor whites who are employed in the low-status occupations of service work, there was little, if any, difference in the education of blacks and of whites who were, for example, barbers, cooks, hairdressers, practical nurses and waiters (Newman 1978:90). Yet the median family income for black and other minority household heads employed in these and other service occupations in 1976 was one-third less than the median income of whites in these same low-prestige jobs. If race is not an appropriate explanation, why is it that whites of limited educations are paid one-third more than blacks who are as qualified as they are? Newman and associates point out that "blacks had achieved 94 percent of whites' educational position by 1974 and 1975, compared with 79 percent in 1940. But whatever the year, blacks' occupational position did not match their educational position." (Newman 1978:49).

There is social differentiation among blacks as well as among whites in the United States. And the stratification range in terms of median income by occupational groups is similar for both racial populations. Whites, who are professionals and who are at the top of the occupational hierarchy, receive a median annual income that is approximately twice as much as that received by whites who are poor. And blacks, who are professionals, receive a median annual income that is about twice as much as that received by blacks who are poor. Because the range of the stratification hierarchy, as defined here, is similar for both racial populations, why is it that only one out of every ten whites is poor compared to around three out of every ten blacks? The differential rate of poverty between blacks and whites cannot be explained as being a function of the increased social class differentiation of the black population when the white population is differentiated just as much as the blacks and has experienced social class differentiation even longer than the blacks. Despite the differentiation of the white population by social class, its rate of poverty has continued to decrease. Thus, the social class differentiation of a population is no impediment to reducing the size of its under-class, as Wilson has suggested.

The clinical or case-study evidence derived from press reports and the findings from scientific surveys lead to the conclusions that race continues to be significant in the United States; that federal laws such as the Civil Rights Act of 1964 and the Voting Rights Act of 1965 are beginning to have an effect because of recent enforcement efforts of the Justice Department but that they have not come near to eliminating split labor markets or local elections that divide along racial lines; and that the new racial battleground shaping up for the future has to do with political control of local governments in which single-member district elections are advocated by black and by brown populations to wrest control from whites and at-large elections and city-county consolidation of institutions such as schools and government are advocated by some whites as a means of retaining control. Finally, this analysis has suggested that racial discrimination rather than a limited education is what holds blacks back and contributes to inequality in employment and income.

We come now to the point of determining what this all means in terms of race relations. To recapitulate, a major daily newspaper wishes to retire from our language and common usage the words racist and racism because — it asserts — they are no longer descriptive of race relations in this nation. The white mayor of a big city criticizes a court decision that sanctions a 10 percent reservation of public works programs for minority contractors and attempts to resist a court order that requires the hiring of minorities in a police department that had one of the lowest percentages of minorities in the country. A federal judge states that a finding of discrimination in the hiring of women and minorities for high-level court jobs is more accurate than inaccurate. A major bank in which racial minorities are less than 1 percent of its work force at the managerial level claims that it has not been remiss in hiring and promoting people in black and in brown racial populations. The first black mayor to win an election in a large Alabama city is supported by only one out of every ten white voters.

These facts appear to indicate that most individuals of the majority race have little, if any, feelings of guilt about the unfair ways that racial minorities have been treated in this nation. In this connection guilt is to the social system what pain is to the organic system—a signal that something is amiss, a warning that something is wrong. By acknowledging pain and dealing with that which caused it, corrective action can be taken in time to prevent permanent harm to the organic system. To suppress pain is to deal with the symptom rather than with the cause. Likewise, if we acknowledge and accept guilt as a signal that something is wrong in the social system and take appropriate corrective actions, we may avoid permanent damage of our society. Both the suppression of pain and the repression of guilt can be fatal.

The continuing significance of race is that it is one of the most sensitive and sure indicators of the presence or absence of justice in our society. To repress the guilt of racial discrimination through denial and other means is to permit injustice to fester and erupt from time to time in race riots and other forms of rebellion.

Our society has not learned how to deal with guilt because it has not learned how to listen to minorities who experience the conditions that should stimulate guilt. Those who are best capable of helping a society to expiate its guilt are those who suffer because of injustice -- the minorities. However, our society will listen to minorities only when they think and speak like the majority.

Years ago in the *New York Times Magazine,* Arthur Schlesinger, Jr. wrote this: "So let us listen more carefully to our losers. A revolution does not have to succeed to make a point. Victory does not render a [person] infallible nor [one's] ideas invincible. 'Success,' said Nietzsche, 'has always been a great liar' " (Schlesinger 1972:62).

Meditating upon success and failure, Theodore Isaac Rubin, the psychiatrist, said: "We must fight for the right to lose. If we don't accept the right to lose, then we so fear failure that we curtail realistic and attainable desires.... But despite this obvious reality, our culture stands rigidly against failure and loss, looks upon loss ... as an insult to the human condition" (Rubin 1975:206). For this reason, we defer to those in charge — members of the majority — and will not listen to those who are subdominant, our many minorities. As Schlesinger said, let us listen more carefully to our losers. They, in the end, may be our salvation.

REFERENCES

Boston Globe. 1980. "Police Set Five-Year Goal: 27 New Black Sergeants." July 10: 16.

Boston Globe. 1979. "Birmingham, The End Of 'Never.'" November 2: 14.

Brink, Williams, and Louis Harris. 1966. *Black and White.* New York: Simon and Schuster.

U.S. Civil Rights Commission, 1978. *Social Indicators of Equality for Minorities and Women.* Washington, D.C.: U.S. Government Printing Office.

Dallas Morning News. 1979. *"Racist, Schmaist."* September 23.

Fletcher, Joseph. 1966. *Situation Ethics.* Philadelphia: Westminster Press.

Keniston, Kenneth, et al. 1977. *All Our Children.* New York: Harcourt Brace Jovanovich.

Margolis, Richard. 1979. "If We Won, Why Aren't We Smiling." In *The Caste and Class Controversy,* edited by C. V. Willie. Dix Hills, N.Y.: General Hall.

Newman, Dorothy K. 1978. "Unclass: An Appraisal." In *The Caste and Class Controversy,* edited by C. V. Willie. Dix Hills, N.Y.: General Hall.

New York Times. 1980. July 15: Letter by Dorothy J. Samuels, Executive Director, New York Civil Liberties Union; July 9: "Cincinnati Police To Hire More Blacks And Women," A12; June 1: "Courts' Own Data Show Minority Job Exclusion," 44.

New York Times. 1979. November 5: "Dallas Suit On Job Bias Is Viewed As Far Reaching," A17; November 1: "Birmingham Victor Elated And Determined," A18; November 1: "Minorities' Influence Will Rise Next Week In Houston's Election," B24.

Rawls, John. 1971. *A Theory of Justice.* Cambridge, M.A.: Harvard University Press.

Rubin, Theodore Isaac. 1975. *Compassion and Self-Hate.* New York: Ballantine Books.

Schlesinger, Jr., Arthur. 1972. "The Power Of Positive Losing." *New York Times Magazine* (June 22).

Sloan, Lee and Robert M. French. 1977. "Black Rule In The Urban South?" In *Black/Brown/White Relations,* edited by C. V. Willie. New Brunswick, N.J.: Transaction Books.

Tournier, Paul. 1962. *Guilt and Grace.* New York: Harper and Row (first published in 1958).

U. S. Census Bureau. 1978. *Money Income in 1979 of Family and Persons in the United States.* P-60, no. 114. Washington, D.C.: U. S. Government Printing Office. July.

Willie, Charles V. 1980. *Leadership Development for Minorities: An Evaluation of a Rockefeller Foundation Program* June.

Wilson, William Julius. 1978. *The Declining Significance of Race.* Chicago: University of Chicago Press.

Chapter **6** SIGNIFICANCE OF RACE
IN THE 1980s

" 'My daddy was a blue-eyed man,' swears black-eyed, white skinned Susie Guillroy Phipps, a ... southern belle ... from southwest Louisiana ..."

"[Mrs.] Phipps ... says she was 'raised white' and 'even married white twice' ... [F]ive years ago ... she drove 230 miles to the Bureau of Vital Statistics [in New Orleans] to get a copy of her birth certificate for a passport application.... [T]he document listed her parents as ... colored."

" 'It took me for a spin,' [Mrs.] Phipps recalled. 'I told the lady it was wrong. My parents were white.... I was sick for two weeks. If I'd had a heart problem, I think I would have had a heart attack.' "

"[S]he hired a lawyer, who filed suit asking that the record be changed and that a state law ... defining as black anyone with [a fraction of] 1/32 'Negro blood' be declared unconstitutional..."

"[A] state magistrate upheld the ... law ... and declined to change [Mrs.] Phipps' birth certificate ... [because] she is the great-great-great-great-great grand-daughter of a black slave woman and a white planter...." (Ben Bradley 1982:2).

Langston Hughes concluded that black blood is really powerful since all it takes is one drop to make you black (quoted Bradley 1982:2).

The president of the Louisiana NAACP (National Association for the Advancement of Colored People) called attention to the Creole ancestry of many people in Louisiana and said that state has the blackest white people and the whitest black people (quoted in Bradley 1982:2).

To Mrs. Phipps, these all may be bad jokes. They probably would not be funny to her. Already she has spent several thousands of dollars on this case. In a decisive way, Mrs. Phipps said, "I don't want to be what I'm not; and I'm not black" (quoted in Bradley 1982:2).

Race is one of the most sensitive and sure indicators of the presence or absence of justice in our society. To repress the guilt of racial discrimination through denial and other means is to permit injustice to fester and erupt from time to time in race riots and other forms of rebellion.

Our society has not learned how to deal with guilt because it has not learned how to listen to minorities who experience the conditions that should stimulate guilt. Those who are most capable of helping a society to expiate its guilt are those who suffer because of injustice — the minorities. However, our society tends to listen to minorities only when they think and speak like the majority.

Guilt is to the social system what pain is to the organic system — a signal that something is amiss, a warning that something is wrong. By acknowledging pain and dealing with that which caused it, corrective action can be taken in time to prevent permanent harm to the organic system. To suppress pain is to deal with the symptom rather than with the cause. Likewise, if we acknowledge and accept guilt as a signal that something is wrong in the social system and take appropriate corrective actions, we may avoid permanent damage to our society. Both the suppression of pain and the repression of guilt can be fatal.

Reflecting upon the bus boycott in Montgomery, Alabama that launched the direct-action phase of the modern civil rights movement, Martin Luther King, Jr. said that discrimination "scars the soul and degrades the personality:" it creates within some whites a false sense of superiority and among some blacks a false sense of inferiority (King 1958:37). These false beliefs encourage the dominance of one group over another.

The family life of black people in the United States can be classified as subdominant in the community power structure. Whites control a disproportionate amount of the nation's resources and the result is that the customs and conventions of whites are inappropriately considered normative for the total society.

In biblical literature, the scapegoat is an animal upon whose head the sins of the people are symbolically placed. Such an animal is then ceremonially sent out or exiled into the wilderness as a way of expiating the community of its evil deeds. In our contemporary communities, black families bear the blame of others as scapegoats through the irrational hostility and guilt of whites.

Whites have projected their own fears upon blacks and black families. A more objective analysis of the status of black families is possible when we recognize that the increasing concern about black families represents not so much a new and unique pathological adaptation of blacks as it does a projection upon blacks of the concerns about the pathological adaptations increasingly found among whites and all families. We know, of course, that the practice of scapegoating is harmful and unethical.

Growing affluence is a fact of life within the black population that has been recognized by a range of scholars, including William Wilson (1978) and Reynolds Farley (1984). In income, occupational opportunity, and educational attainment, Farley reports definite improvement among black households. The gap in median school years completed between black and white groups has been substantially reduced; the proportion of blacks in prestigious and higher-paying jobs has increased; and black earnings have improved (Farley 1984:194-195). E. Franklin Frazier reported in an article published near the midpoint of the twentieth century that only approximately one-eighth of black families were able to maintain a middle-class way of life (Frazier 1968:207).

Some social scientists, such as Wilson, have linked "the improving position of the black middle class" to an alleged "worsening condition of the black under-class" (Wilson 1987: ix, vii). The Wilson analysis, however, is flawed on two counts: it does not demonstrate that poverty among blacks is increasing and it does not provide a logical explanation of how improvement in one sector of the black population is harmful to another.

We know from an analysis of data published by the U.S. Bureau of the Census over the years that the proportion of black and of white families below the poverty line has been reduced. Three decades ago, one-sixth of all whites in families were poor. Today, the proportion is approximately 10 percent (U.S. Bureau of the Census 1985:455). The ratio of the poor in these racial populations has remained more or less constant over the years, although the proportion of the poor has diminished. The proportion of black poor was 3.4 times higher than the proportion of white poor three decades ago and is 3.3 times greater today. These data indicate that although the size of the poor population in both groups has decreased, the condition of the black poor with reference to the white poor has not worsened. Neither has the condition of the black poor with reference to the white poor improved over the years. As stated above, the ratios for the two different time periods have remained more or less the same. Thus, there is no decline in the significance of race as a circumstantial factor in poverty.

Even when the analysis is limited to an examination of indicators for blacks only, Farley states that "it is an oversimplification to claim that the black community is now split into an elite and an under-class" (Farley 1984:190). With reference to education, he found that "lower-class blacks are not falling further behind upper-class blacks" (Farley 1984:177). Moreover, Farley reports that the distribution of family income within the black population has changed very little over the last thirty years: "the richest five percent of black families have received about 16 percent of all the income obtained by black families, while the poorest 20 percent of black families have received about 4 percent" (Farley 1984:191). These data indicated that racial discrimination is a constant experience in the United States and probably accounts for continuing differentials in status position between blacks and whites; that the proportional size of the poor population has declined among both racial groups; and that improvements among some sectors of the black population have not contributed to a worsened condition among other sectors of the black population.

The analysis thus far confirms the assertion by Martin Luther King, Jr., that "we are caught in a network of inescapable mutuality" (King 1958:199). An analysis of the civil rights movement reveals linkages between affluent and poor blacks have been helpful rather than harmful. Based on an examination of successful educational reform initiatives among blacks, such as those for school desegregation, it appears that "a subdominant population is likely to intensify its press for affirmative action with reference to equal access and equitable distribution of community resources when it grows in numbers from a small minority to a larger and heterogeneous population.... The size of a population and its socioeconomic differentiation are interrelated phenomena that must be examined to determine their joint effect if the pattern of the press for social action by a subdominant population is to be understood" (Willie 1983: 197).

If a diversified population is essential in social action efforts among blacks and other subdominant populations, then a one-sided analysis that focuses only on the poor or lower-class or under-class among blacks is a perspective that is too limited for the formulation of adequate public policy. A fundamental fact about black contemporary life is the increasing socioeconomic differentiation found among such households in the United States. This is a fact that should be celebrated.

With reference to income, the interracial distribution for black and for white families has manifested only a modest change over the years in a positive direction favorable to blacks. The ratio of black to white median family income was .54 in 1950 before the Brown (Supreme Court) decision that outlawed segregation and .56 slightly more than three decades later (in 1983 constant dollars). This ratio represented a slight gain of only 2 percentage points in median annual income for all black families in comparison with such income for all white families (U.S. Bureau of the Census 1985:446). During nearly a quarter of a century, beginning in 1959, blacks—whose proportion of poor was three and two-fifths times greater than that for whites in 1959—continued at only a slightly reduced differential of three and one-third times greater in 1982 (U.S. Bureau of the Census 1985:455).

Despite the more or less constant ratio of the association of black to white annual family income when studied by a central tendency measure like the median, analysis of the income range reveals substantial improvements favorable to blacks. A ratio of the proportion of black families with incomes in the lowest quintile of the range in 1954 was 2.17 times greater than the proportion of whites similarly situated. However, in 1977 (nearly a quarter of a century later), the ratio of the proportions for these two populations was down to 1.98. In the highest quintile of family income, the ratio of the proportion of blacks to whites at this income level was only .27 in 1954. By 1977, the ratio of the proportion of blacks to whites in the highest fifth of the income range had increased to .47. The actual proportion of blacks and other races in the bottom fifth of the family-income hierarchy decreased from 43.3 percent in 1954 to 39.6 percent in 1977; in the top fifth of the family-income hierarchy, the proportion of blacks and other races increased from 5.3 percent in 1954 to 9.4 percent in 1977. Data were not analyzed for the 1980s but probably reflect the same pattern of the past two decades (U.S. Bureau of the Census 1980:483).

While black families continue to have a higher proportion of their population in the low-income range and a lower proportion of their population in the high-income range compared with white families, the proportion of blacks in the bottom quintile has decreased while the proportion of blacks in the top quintiles has increased. While these findings represent a severe judgment upon our society and its continuing discriminatory practice in the distribution of income among families of different racial groups, they also confirm that poverty among blacks and all families has decreased and that affluence among blacks and all families has increased. Moreover, this analysis indicates the importance of studying the prevalence rate of families by race for the entire range of income categories rather than focusing only on measures of central tendency such as the mean, median, or mode. This analysis reveals that race has not declined but continues as a significant variable differentiating blacks from whites at all income levels and that the proportion of poor black families has decreased while the proportions of affluent black families has increased. Thus, the condition of lower-class blacks has not worsened as the condition of middle-class blacks has improved, as claimed by Wilson in his book, *The Truly Disadvantaged* (1987: vii).

With reference to employment, the proportion of white males and black males who work in the most prestigious professional-technical, managerial-administrative jobs had only modest increases during the past decade. White males in these occupational categories varied from 28 percent of the white employed population over sixteen years of age in 1972 to 30.5 percent of such workers in the race in 1979—an increase of 2.5 percentage points. Black males and those of other races exhibited a similiar rate of change for these occupations; they increased from 13 percent of those employed sixteen years of age or older who worked in these most prestigious jobs in 1972 to 17.4 percent in 1979—an increase of 4.4 percentage points (U.S. Bureau of Labor Statistics 1980:46-48). The ratio of these proportions of blacks and whites at the top of the occupational hierarchy changed slightly in a direction that favored blacks and other races. The increase in the racial ratio ranged from .46, in 1972, to .57, the final year of the decade.

For the bottom of the occupational hierarchy, the decade of the seventies showed slight changes that also favored blacks and other racial minorities. While the proportion of white males sixteen or older who worked as laborers, private household workers, and service workers remained constant at 15.9 percent in 1972 and 1979, the proportion of black males and employed males of other races in these least prestigious jobs dropped slightly from 36 percent in 1972 to 31.4 percent in 1979 (U.S. Bureau of Labor Statistics 1980:46–48). The racial ratio of the proportion of black males to white males at the bottom of the occupational hierarchy moved from 2.26 in 1972 down to 1.95 in 1979.

Again, when racial difference is analyzed, it is shown to continue as a mediating force in inequitable distribution of jobs. At the close of the 1970s, for example, the proportion of professional and managerial workers among white males (30.5 percent) was nearly twice as great as the proportion of such workers employed as laborers and service workers (15.9 percent). The converse was true for black males; their proportion

of laborers and service workers (31.4 percent) was nearly twice
as great as the proportion of professional and managerial
workers (17.4 percent). Nevertheless, there was a change for
blacks both at the top and the bottom of the occupational
hierarchy. The modest increase in the proportion of blacks who
got high-income jobs during the 1970s was accompanied by a
modest decrease in black workers in low-income jobs. Apparently, help for affluent blacks did not harm poor blacks as
claimed by William Wilson (1978, 1987).

   The disadvantaged circumstances that black families have
experienced as participants in the labor force in the United
States is not simply a result of inadequate education, another
Wilson contention (1978:104–9). A majority of all adults
twenty-five years of age and over in black and in white racial
populations are high school graduates. The median school years
completed by blacks and whites differs by only a few months today compared to a difference of 2.5 years in 1950 (U.S. Bureau
of the Census 1985:134). Nevertheless, whites had a median
family income that fluctuated from 40 to 45 percent greater
than the median for blacks during the first half of the 1980
decade (U.S. Bureau of the Census 1985:134).

   To test the Wilson hypothesis that low-income black households are locked into the low-wage sector because of their inadequate education, a ratio was computed of the median family income of poorly educated blacks (those with less than a grade
school education) and the median family income of poorly
educated whites. Poorly educated blacks in 1982 earned 23 percent less than the income received by poorly educated whites.
The same pattern persisted for highly educated blacks who are
college graduates; they earned 22 percent less than the income
received by highly educated whites. The ratios of .77 and .78,
respectively, for these pairs of least- and most-educated households among blacks and whites are almost identical (U.S. Bureau
of the Census 1985:447). The diminishing gap in educational
achievement between the races has not brought with it equitable
employment and earning experiences; inequity that is racially
based remains.

Despite their continuing experience of discrimination, black families are upwardly mobile. During the first half of the 1980s, 9.5 percent of the blacks twenty-five years old and over had graduated from college (compared to 18 percent for the total population); 13 percent of blacks sixteen years of age and over were employed as managers and professionals (compared to 22 percent of the total population); and 2.6 percent of black households earned $50,000 or more each year (compared to 10.9 percent of the total population) (U.S. Bureau of the Census 1985:134, 402, 445).

Education may be conceptualized as an input variable, occupation as a process variable, and income as an outcome variable. If these three are interrelated, then what one earns is a function of the kind of work one performs. And the kind of work one performs is based on educational attainment. High-level education as an input variable should beget high-level employment as a process variable which, in turn, should result in high-level income. Blacks in families lag behind the population at large as participants in the highest levels of educational and occupational attainment; their participation rate is approximately 40 to 50 percent less than others. This means that the proportion of blacks in the highest income level should also be approximately 40 to 50 percent less than that for the population at large. Actually, blacks lag behind others in the proportion who received highest income by approximately three-quarters. The penalty which blacks experience in reduced numbers who receive the highest income is disproportionate to their participation rate in the highest levels of occupational and educational attainment. This disproportionality is a sign of continuing racial discrimination.

Although the proportion of black families in the first income quintile (the lowest) is twice as great as it should be and the proportion in the fifth income quintile (the highest) is one-half less than it ought to be — if such families were distributed equally (U.S. Bureau of the Census 1980:483), blacks, nevertheless, have made progress as participants in the economy at all income levels. The black population is no longer homogeneously poor.

Some social scientists view with alarm this increasing diversity as having the possibility of polarizing the population. Actually, the opposite is likely to occur. A diversified population is more capable of cooperating and adapting to changing circumstances because of the presence of multiple resources and complementary talents.

From population genetics we learn that "a species [is] polymorphic if it contains a variety of genotypes, each of which is superior in adaptive value to the others ... in the territory occupied...." Moreover, population genetics reveal that "polymorphic populations [are], in general, more efficient in the exploitation of ... opportunities of an environment than genetically uniform ones...." (Dobzhansky 1951:132–33). Thus, the increasing diversity of black families in the United States is not a liability but a sociological asset.

In *Stride Toward Freedom,* Martin Luther King, Jr. described how a diversified black population worked together and eliminated segregated seating in the city public transportation system of Montgomery, Alabama, in the 1950s. He said the mass meetings associated with this movement cut across class lines. They brought together "working people" and "professionals." He described the Montgomery bus boycott by blacks as bringing together "men and women who had been separated from each other by false standards of class." They cooperated with each other in a "common struggle for freedom and human dignity" (King 1958:86). The struggle continues for black families at all levels of social organization. The *New York Times* reports that "racial discrimination is a significant contributor to the disproportionate number of blacks in the underclass" (Wilkerson 1987:26).

There is ample evidence that family income varies by race, on the one hand, and that family stability correlates positively with household disposable income, on the other hand. A plausible explanation of the different rates of family stability found among blacks and whites, therefore, would seem to be the different economic circumstances experienced by the two racial populations. And their different economic circumstances, according to economist Herman Miller, are largely due to racial discrimination. He said "the average [black] earns less than the average white, even when he has the same years of schooling and does the same kind of work" (Miller 1964:21).

Well into the 1980s the median income figures for blacks and whites demonstrated the absence of parity. The median for blacks hovered around 55 percent of that received by whites (U.S. Bureau of the Census 1985:32). Thus, the difference between the proportion of white families (84.7 percent in 1983) and the proportion of black families (53.4 percent in 1983) who lived in married, two-parent units is probably a function of unequal income rather than cultural norms.

We know, for example, that affluent households have a higher probability of being two-parent families than poor households. More than three-fourths of black as well as white households in the United States with incomes above $25,000 (in 1983) were husband-wife families. While half of the whites were in the top half of the income range and earned more than $25,000, only one-fourth of blacks had such income (Farley and Allen 1987:174–75). It is reasonable to assume that if more blacks were in the top half of the economic scale, more would live in two-parent households.

Evidence also shows that a majority of poor whites as well as poor blacks with income below the federal poverty line live in single-parent or single-person households (Farley and Allen 1987:174–75). However, only 10.6 percent of white persons are poor compared to 34.9 percent of black persons (U.S. Bureau of the Census 1985:455). Since family instability is associated with low-income status, it is reasonable to assume that a higher proportion of white families than is presently seen would be unstable if a higher proportion of white persons were poor.

On the basis of this analysis, one may conclude that racial discrimination and its negative effects upon the economic status of blacks make a substantial contribution to their higher rate of family instability compared to whites and that cultural differences, if any, are of limited value in explaining differential rates of family instability among racial populations in the United States.

The black family is undergoing profound change in a society in great flux. We must recognize that—as an institution—the black family is under siege from a dominant culture that is alternately indifferent or hostile.

That black families survive is testimony to their strength, endurance and adaptability. Survival, however, is not a goal but a means. The challenge to the black community and the nation at large is to build upon survival strengths and continue to lay the groundwork for black achievement and full participation in all aspects of American life.

REFERENCES

Bradley, Ben. 1982. "Louisiana Legal System Grapples With Old Issue Of Blood And Race," *Boston Globe* September 18: 2.

Dobzhansky, Theodosius. 1951. *Genetics and the Origins of the Species.* New York: Columbia University Press.

Farley, Reynolds. 1984. *Blacks and Whites.* Cambridge, M.A.: Harvard University Press.

Farley, Reynolds and Walter R. Allen. 1987. *The Color Line and the Quality of Life in America.* New York: Russell Sage Foundation.

Frazier, E. Franklin. 1968. "The Negro Family In America." In *Franklin Frazier on Race Relations,* edited by G. Franklin Edwards. Chicago: University of Chicago Press.

Keniston, Kenneth. 1977. *All Our Children.* New York: Harcourt Brace Jovanovich.

King, Martin Luther, Jr. 1958. *Stride Toward Freedom.* New York: Harper and Row.

Miller, Herman. 1964. *Rich Man, Poor Man.* New York: Crowell.

U.S. Bureau of the Census. 1980. *Social Indicators III.* Washington, D.C.: U.S. Government Printing Office.

U.S. Bureau of the Census. 1985. *Statistical Abstract of the United States.* Washington, D.C.: U.S. Government Printing Office.

U.S. Bureau of Labor Statistics. 1980. *Handbook of Labor Statistics.* Washington, D.C.: U.S. Government Printing Office.

Wilkerson, Isabel. 1987. "Growth of the Very Poor is Focus of New Studies," *New York Times* December 20: 26.

Willie, Charles Vert. 1983. *Race, Ethnicity and Socioeconomic Status.* Dix Hills, N.Y.: General Hall.

_____. 1985. *Black and White Families.* Dix Hills, N.Y.: General Hall.

Wilson, William Julius. 1978. *The Declining Significance of Race.* Chicago: University of Chicago Press.

_____. 1987. *The Truly Disadvantaged.* Chicago: University of Chicago Press.

PART III

COMMENTARY ON THE DECLINING SIGNIFICANCE OF RACE

Chapter **7** IF WE WON,
WHY AREN'T WE SMILING?*

Richard Margolis

A review for *Change,* April 1979 of *The Declining Significance of Race: Blacks and Changing American Institutions* by William Julius Wilson, University of Chicago and *Protest, Politics and Prosperity: Black Americans and White Institutions, 1940–75* by Dorothy K. Newman, et al. New York: Pantheon.

The near-ubiquity of white racism in America has long been an open secret but not until relatively recent times has it been widely perceived as a social problem. Chief Justice Roger Brook Taney, in his now notorious Dred Scott decision (1857), doubtless spoke for most white citizens of his day when, without a trace of bad conscience, he approvingly thumbnailed the history of American racism. "For more than a century before the Declaration of Independence," the Chief Justice noted, "the Negroes had been regarded as beings of an inferior order ... so far inferior that they had no rights which a white man was bound to respect." In those times of moral certitude and for generations to come, the notion of "Negro inferiority" was not so much an issue as it was an axiom. Journalists diligently reported it; commentators soberly confirmed it; scholars ponderously "proved" it. So embedded in the national psyche was white hubris that the pop historian Hendrik Van Loon, in a 1923 award-winning essay on "Tolerance," could casually observe that "a Zulu riding in a Rolls Royce is still a Zulu." (Uncle Remus back then professed a larger vision: "Niggers is niggers now, but de time wuz w'en we 'uz all niggers tergedder.")

Very likely it wasn't until the 1930s that people in any large numbers began to see something ugly in all that arrogance and to suspect that the white emperor wore no clothes. For many, Gunnar Myrdal made the new consciousness official with his opening lines to *An American Dilemma* (1944): "There is a 'Negro problem' in the United States," he wrote, "and most Americans are aware of it.... Americans have to react to it, politically as citizens and ... privately as neighbors." As Myrdal and his coauthors made clear in that large and seminal work, the "Negro problem" was really a white problem; for they demonstrated beyond cavil the extent to which we had institutionalized racial discrimination, weaving it tightly — perhaps inextricably — into the fabric of our national life. This we did in defiance of what Myrdal called "the American Creed" by which he meant that shared set of beliefs roughly embodied in the first phrases of the Declaration of Independence. It was his opinion that the resulting clash between the ideal of equality and the ideology of racism had made a battleground of our collective conscience. "America," he wrote," is continuously struggling for its soul."

So — how now goes the struggle? From the two books at hand we get two different answers, as well as two different temperatures of scholarship. William Julius Wilson, a black sociologist at the University of Chicago, is cool, theoretical, and dispassionate in tone. Using history as his guide and various economic theories as his goal, Wilson attempts to persuade us that the very boundaries of the struggle have lately shifted and that Myrdal's "Negro problem" is now largely extinct; what we have instead is a class problem, wherein a sizable and enduring black under-class finds itself the victim, not of racist tradition, but of technological progress. That this youthful army of the unemployed happens to be black, says Wilson, is "an accident of history" rather than a consequence of continuing white discrimination.

Dorothy K. Newman is also a sociologist, one who spent years plumbing the empirical depths of segregation as research director of the National Urban League. Compared with Wilson, Newman and her author-colleagues are hot, pragmatic, and compassionate. While their book, billed as a thirty-five year up-date of Myrdal, perfunctorily affirms the gains blacks have made since the early sixties, it concentrates more on the gains they have not made, citing time and again "the resistance of white Americans to accepting blacks as equals." The message is that white racism remains alive and well and that the American soul struggle is still up for grabs.

Both these books have been out long enough now to have attracted their partisans and their reprovers; and, if my periodical readings are a fair sample, it seems clear that in the war of reviews, Wilson has won hands down. Even The *New York Times,* not the world's most roseate journal, considered Wilson's sophisticated optimism more convincing than Newman's straight-forward gloom. Yet Newman, for all her old-fashioned, civil-righter's biases, surely has a firmer grip on current racial realities than does Wilson. (Here I should mention a "conflict of interest:" I was lucky enough to read an early draft of the Newman manuscript and to make some minor suggestions).

If most reviewers have preferred Wilson's bright mirage to Newman's dark mirror, it may be because they, like the rest of us, are weary of domestic strife and of guilt-edged sermons. Many Americans these days are understandably eager to accept glad racial tidings with no questions asked, especially when they come to us courtesy of a brilliant black scholar with a taste for abstractions. Pangloss, it turns out, is a master theoretician.

In *The Declining Significance of Race,* Wilson ranges freely and fascinatingly over the history of racial oppression in the United States—from pre-Civil War days, when the estates of white southern aristocrats were irrigated by the sweat of black slaves, to pre-New Deal days, when northern industrialists and their white workers frequently combined to shut blacks out of the job market. (Except during strikes: Wilson includes a startling table showing the extent to which corporations, between 1916 and 1934, relied on scab black labor to bust lily-white unions).

His history is largely economic; although he says he does not subscribe to "the view that racial problems are necessarily derived from more fundamental class problems," he has, nonetheless, made a central issue of the constantly shifting job market, persuasively linking the course of racism to the aspirations of white capitalists and to the fears of white workers. No one has done this better or more tellingly. Wilson is able to establish, for example, that the late nineteenth century was for the North "an unprecedented period of racial unity and integration," distinguished by relatively equal employment opportunities and by the passage in several states of civil rights legislation. Only later, when southern blacks began to drift northward in large numbers, did frightened whites repeal the laws and lock the factory gates.

Old patterns of economic discrimination, says Wilson, began to break up with the New Deal, when the more liberal unions lowered the color bar a notch or two. The production demands of World War II, followed by two decades of nearly uninterrupted prosperity, further eroded Jim Crowism in the North. Finally, the protests and civil rights reforms of the sixties completed the progressive cycle begun almost half a century ago and brought us, in Wilson's view, to our present nonracial impasse.

He devotes considerable space in support of his proposition that there are now two classes of black Americans — the uneducated poor and the educated affluent — where before there had been only one (all poor). Middle-class blacks, he argues, are doing just fine, thanks to the new, nondiscriminatory job market; lower-class blacks, meanwhile, suffer hardships that are largely unrelated to race. These ghetto dwellers, says Wilson, simply have had the ill luck to have come to age at the wrong moment — when the economy is slowing down, when factories are automating and when corporations are moving outward from cities to suburbs. Therefore, "It would be nearly impossible to comprehend the economic plight of lower-class blacks in the inner city by focusing solely on racial oppression; that is [on] the overt and explicit effort of whites to keep blacks in a subjugated state...."

And: "It would also be difficult to explain the rapid economic improvement of the black elite by rigidly postulating the view that traditional patterns of discrimination are still salient in the labor-market practices of American industries." After which Wilson nails down his main plank: "Economic class is now a more important factor than race in determining job placement for blacks."

Wilson's news has been so cheerfully received because what he seems to be telling us is precisely what we've always longed to hear: that we have managed to slip through the horns of our American Dilemma and that the ancient battle for racial justice is nearly won. But, then, why aren't we dancing in the streets? Is it possible that the report of racism's death has been greatly exaggerated?

Newman's *Protest, Politics and Prosperity* is helpful here. It pitilessly documents our sins and, by coincidence, spotlights some missing beams in Wilson's logical structure. Take the matter of employment, which Newman, like Wilson, thinks central to any discussion of race. In Newman's book, today's labor market for blacks is still no promised land; it remains a white-dominated wilderness, full of prickly prejudices and discriminatory practices. "The black struggle for jobs continues," Newman notes, "because inequality still prevails. Racial discrimination and acceptance of the resulting inequality remain embedded in the white-dominated job market, buttressed by many rationalizations." An accompanying chart bears her out. It compares the rise, from 1940-75, of black occupational positions with those of white workers. True, blacks rose faster than did whites, but as of 1975 blacks had not even reached the whites' 1940 level! Thus, what Wilson would call progress, Newman has labeled disaster.

This book is especially persuasive in two other areas — education and housing. Where Wilson treats these subjects mechanistically, citing inferior schools and neighborhoods as two more nonracial reasons blacks can't get jobs, Newman confronts them squarely as racial issues. She observes, first, that corporations often use such social ills as excuses for continuing racist employment policies and, second, that segregated housing, far from being an economic accident, is part of a broad social intent on the part of white-controlled institutions, including the banks, the real estate industry and some government agencies.

In a chapter on "Learning Without Earning," Newman points to industry's new, credential-ridden job standards which compel prospective employees to seek college degrees in order to "learn" how to perform tasks that, in the past, have been adequately handled by persons who never finished high school; and she suggests that such credentialism is really a smoke screen for racism—a respectable device allowing corporations to shun blacks without seeming to violate the tenets of affirmative action. Perhaps she carries the point too far; still, her approach is refreshingly tough-minded in contrast to Wilson's easy acceptance of corporate rationales.

Likewise, in a chapter called "But Not Next Door," Newman and her coauthors are able to demonstrate that housing is "one of the areas of greatest white resistance to integration," that, since 1960, neighborhood segregation has grown worse and that federal policy has been of little or no use in loosening the suburban noose that chokes the black inner-city. Newman correctly suggests that polite, white, suburban racism—pampered by zoning exclusions and financed by the taxes of newly located industries—comes very close to the heart of the employment problem. As Patricia Harris, Secretary of the Department of Housing and Urban Development, has observed, "Communities that say we will take the benefit of a good tax base but will not let people, who might benefit from that employment, live in this community ought to be required to think about the injustice of that."

Ultimately, for all its strengths, the Wilson book works to postpone that elusive moment of truth for white Americans while the Newman book tries to keep us struggling toward the light. It appears we have miles to go before our soul awakes.

Chapter **8** CAMOUFLAGING THE COLOR
LINE: A CRITIQUE*

Harry Edwards, University of
California-Berkeley

A review prepared for *Social Forces,* April 1979, of *The Declining
Significance of Race* by William Julius Wilson.

William Wilson's latest book demonstrates, once again, the
value of calculated, evocative packaging and promotion — or, in
marketing lingo, "HYPE" — in advancing a product that, otherwise, might generate far less than extraordinary attention, much
less opportunistic commendation. Under cover of a highly provocative and controversial title, the author presents a basically
mediocre work that is, both, incredibly tendentious and critically
deficient, empirically and theoretically. All too often, not only
does he fail to persuasively substantiate his contentions but many
of his inferences and conclusions are so discrepant relative to
"supportive" evidence that the former are reduced to non-
sequiturs. And, most unfortunately, the author is, apparently,
quite content to summarily dismiss troublesome potential and
existing structural and sociopolitical developments threatening
the fundamental credibility of his central thesis, i.e., that in
America's modern industrial era, economic class position, not
race, has emerged as the major determinant of black life
chances. The validity of his contention hinges upon the viability
of a series of explicitly stipulated circumstances whose presumed

101

integrity has been highly questionable for some years now and which, further, show every sign of accelerated deterioration.

The following constitute the critically imperative foundations of Wilson's argument:

1. The existence of expanding high-wage, high-status job opportunities in both the corporate and government sectors (pp. 88, 97-104, 109-11, 120-21, 150-54);

2. The forceful intervention of the state to remove contemporary racist obstacles and to rectify the historical legacy of artificially discriminatory barriers to employment opportunities through court action, occupational rights legislation, and executive orders (such as Executive Order 11246 which mandated affirmative action programs) (p. 150);

3. The existence of a powerful political and social movement against job discrimination (pp. 134-41, 153);

4. The existence of stable, if not expanding, access by minorities to higher education and advanced technological training opportunities (pp. 18-121).

Any substantial deterioration in the optimal character of any one of these critical circumstances would seriously impune the integrity of the author's analysis by his own admission. Nevertheless, he fails to even cite—much less systematically address—widely published and acknowledged evidence to the effect that all four circumstances have deteriorated significantly; and his cavalier response to a purely suppositious question regarding the deterioration of circumstance 1., above, is that "... although it is possible that an economic disaster could produce racial competition for higher paying jobs and white efforts to exclude talented blacks, it is difficult to entertain this idea as a real possibility *in the face of the powerful political and social movement against job discrimination ... there is little available evidence to suggest that the economic gains of privileged blacks will be reversed...* " (p. 153, emphasis added).

Such "non-responses" unavoidably reflect upon the level of veracity, naivete, or both exhibited in the book, especially given the contextual genesis and implications of such structural and sociopolitical phenomena as the Bakke and Weber cases; the precipitous decline in black college enrollment as well as black faculty and staff recruitment since 1971; the scores of individual and class-action assaults by whites against affirmative action programs; the increasing neglect of both affirmative action compliance and enforcement nationwide—particularly as these apply to high-wage, high-status job positions; the passage of Proposition 13 in California and the increasing signs of a growing "tax revolt" nationally; "stagflation;" and the energy crisis—just to cite a few well-known and highly documented mitigating considerations. These factors have already contributed toward not only halting but reversing economic gains at all levels of black society—particularly those accruing to the black middle class. Indeed, according to both this book and one of Wilson's earlier works, the mere potential competitiveness of minorities in an economic environment characterized by declining expectations (not to speak of actual deterioration) has historically been sufficient to generate a shift from inter-individual to inter-racial competition and even conflict—particularly over scarce, highly valued rewards.

The credibility of the work is also vulnerable on other grounds. Far too frequently the author posits conclusions and inferences that are substantially idiosyncratic or simply irrelevant to "supporting" data. For example, I find the empirical data presented in the second paragraph, page 114, far too general and unfocused to corroborate his contention that a "rapid rise in the proportion of 'high-cost' disadvantaged students" corresponded to a "drop in overall educational performance in urban public schools." Even more disturbing is the inclusion of utterly superfluous statistics on remedial help required by "half the entering freshmen" at City University of New York following open enrollment.

Similarly, Wilson's conclusions regarding some broad historical analyses leave much to be desired. For instance, conclusions derived from the historical analysis of black-white relations in the pre-industrial, antebellum South fail to encompass the demonstrable possibility that elite slave-owing whites and non-slave owing whites arrived at mutually accommodative economic arrangements — largely at the expense of blacks. Inadequate also is his treatment of black-white relations during the period following the Civil War and before World War II (see Chapters 1-4). While such a track neatly camouflages inadequacies in his analysis, it speaks very poorly for the credibility of the work.

And apparently it is not simply the complex, broad historical concerns that confounded the author's analytical astuteness. On page 24, he resolutely asserts that "... the ownership of slaves was a privilege enjoyed by only a small percentage of free families in the South. *Of the 1,156,000 free southern families in 1860, only 385,000 (roughly one-fourth) owned slaves ...*" (Emphasis added.) His insistence that "roughly" only one-fourth of the free families owned slaves is reiterated on page 45. While his assertion ostensibly supports his claims that slaveowners' political hegemony was based on the structure of the economic system and not upon their proportionate numbers, it also brutalizes elementary mathematical logic. For if 385,000 approximates some "rough" fraction of 1,156,000, it is *one-third,* not *one-fourth.* Given the fact that the author contends (on page 56) that one-third blacks in major cities constitutes a population sufficient to "raise the specter" of black control of cities (even with no discernible economic base, pages 111-17), his argument that the economic structure, alone, was responsible for slaveowner hegemony is severly undermined — even, assuming, that there was hegemony rather than white slaveowner and non-slaveowner mutual accommodation at black expense.

Space limitation will allow for mention of only one other seriously erroneous contention typical of other instances throughout the book. The author's assertion (page 135) that "Lower-class blacks had little involvement in civil rights politics up to the mid-1960s" is almost too ludicrous to comment upon. The statement seriously demeans the contributions of the thousands of domestics, "bus boys," unemployed and underemployed blacks who participated (along with middle-class blacks and sympathetic whites) — often times at great personal risk in bus boycotts, voter registration drives, school desegregation efforts, and countless other non-violent direct action protests throughout the 1950s and 1960s. Again, the statement serves the author's contention that "... Black protest tends often to be a by-product of economic class position ..." as opposed to over riding racial group circumstances but it also flies in the face of documented, historical fact.

Overall, the book should be recommended owing to the character and sheer volume of its limitations rather than for reasons related to any contributions it purports to make. For those seriously interested in the subject matter covered, however, I would strongly suggest consideration of the Carnegie funded study *Protest, Politics and Prosperity: Black Americans and White Institutions,* by Dorothy K. Newman, et al. New York: Pantheon, 1978. Upon any objective appraisal of the evidence and findings presented in this book, as well as others too numerous to cite, one of two conclusions becomes inevitable: 1. far from declining, the significance of race in the life chances of minorities in America is increasing at an accelerating rate; or 2. if the significance of race has declined, it has done so only for working- and middle-class whites owing to their increasing "niggerization" within the context of their intraracial class struggles. Paradoxically, the latter alternative results no less in the maintenance, if not an increase in the significance of race for minorities since they are thrown into greater competition with downwardly mobile whites.

In sum, then, Wilson's work not withstanding, the validity of Dr. DuBois' prophetic observation remains utterly unchallenged: the overwhelmingly significant problem of America in the twentieth century remains "the problem of the color line."

Chapter **9** THE CHANGING —
NOT DECLINING —
SIGNIFICANCE OF RACE*

Thomas F. Pettigrew,
University of California-Santa Cruz

A review for *Contemporary Sociology* of *The Declining Significance of Race: Blacks and Changing American Institutions,* by William Julius Wilson.

From an emphasis on racism in his previous work, William Wilson now asserts the paramount significance of social class. Three facets of this volume must be considered in order to judge his new position: 1. its analysis of black-white relations throughout American history; 2. its intimations of a theoretical alternative to "orthodox Marxist" and split labor-market theory; and 3. its conclusion that the significance of race is declining.

1. Wilson divides American race relations into three historical stages — the preindustrial ("the period of plantation economy and racial-caste oppression" extending to the Civil War), the industrial ("the period of industrial expansion, class conflict and racial oppression" extending from the Civil War to the New Deal), and the modern industrial ("the period of progressive transition from racial ... to class inequalities" extending from World War II to the present). The book then attempts to demonstrate that each stage's unique form of racial interraction was shaped by its distinctive economy and polity.

*Reprinted with permission of the author, *Contemporary Sociology,* and the American Sociological Association.

Such a thesis is hardly groundbreaking. The paternalistic versus competitive modes of the preindustrial and industrial stages follow closely Pierre van den Berghe's well-known dichotomy. And particular secondary sources are relied upon heavily for the descriptions of each stage, especially the writings on slavery by Eugene Genovese, on southern history by Vann Woodward and on black politics by Ira Katznelson and Martin Kilson. Since *The Declining Significance of Race* is barely 50,000 words with considerable repetition, the historical review is, necessarily, highly selective and a bit superficial at points. For example, it is repeatedly asserted that the South's white lower-class alone legalized Jim Crow segregation at the turn of the century (pp. 17, 56-57, 146). This statement fits Wilson's simplified scheme of economic determinism but it ignores the mixed evidence presented by sociological and historical sources. In some states, such as Virginia, the elite was largely responsible and, in others, it was highly implicated.

Nonetheless, Wilson's review presents a brief overview of American racial history that is provocative and engaging if not novel and definitive. But its purpose is more ambitious, for it is proposing a new theoretical perspective.

2. The author outlines two major economic class theories of race relations. "Orthodox Marxists" are said to view racial conflict as a "mask for privilege" that conceals the capitalists' efforts to divide workers and exploit minorities. Oliver Cox, Paul Sweezy, and Michael Reich are among those so categorized. Edna Bonacich's split labor-market theory is cited in opposition to the Marxist position. Instead of associating racial stratification with capitalist manipulations, Bonacich associates it with the higher-paid, white working-class that endeavors to exclude the lower-paid, black working-class. Wilson then tests these rival predictions in his historical descriptions.

Some eras are regarded as consistent with Marxist contentions — slavery in the antebellum South and the short-lived Black Codes immediately following the Civil War. Others appear consistent with split labor-market ideas — racial stratification in the late antebellum North and the postbellum South. But neither theory, Wilson contends, can account for all of these key eras nor are they relevant to the present, modern industrial stage. They fail because they do not focus on the constraints imposed by the particular systems of production in each region and period. And they shed little light on the present period, because they do not focus sufficiently on the polity.

One criticism of this argument is that it attacks incomplete forms of these class theories. Marxists have provided explanations for the rise of Jim Crow. Wilson may not find such explanations persuasive but his abbreviated discussion does not consider them.

A deeper criticism, however, is the book's failure to define an alternative. It is interesting to argue the central importance of particular systems of production; but, without an explicit general statement tying this argument together with testable predictions, there is no theory being offered. Wilson realizes this weakness, for he writes in a footnote:

> Of course, for our purposes, it would be desirable to develop a more comprehensive theory that systematically integrates propositions drawn from the economic class theories. Although I do not attempt such an ambitious project in this book, I do believe that my theoretical arguments have sufficient scope to deal with a variety of historical situations and constitute at least an implicit theory of social change and race relations. (p. 164-65).

But it is precisely this "ambitious project" that would have made the work a major contribution. This recalls the same problem with Wilson's earlier volume. *Power, Racism and Privilege* (New York: MacMillan, 1973) was also a mini-sized descriptive volume that never stated the argument in explicit, testable, theoretical terms. My review of that book (*Social Forces,* 1975, 54, 291-92) closed with a paragraph that equally well fit this one:

> In short, this book represents an interesting initial statement and outline of a broad theoretical ap-

proach.... It needs further specification to be a full-blown theory. One hopes this elaboration will appear in later works by the author. (P. 292.)

3. But, as its attention-provoking title suggests, *The Declining Significance of Race* departs from the earlier work in its conclusion. He maintains that "class has become more important than race in determining black life chances in the modern industrial period" (p. 150). A segmented labor market leads to shrinking opportunities for poorly trained blacks and "unprecedented job opportunities in the growing government and corporate sectors" for well-trained blacks. And, Wilson reasons, the increasing importance of class must signify the decreasing importance of race.

The rapidly increasing stratification within the black world has long been recognized. President Lyndon Johnson made this phenomenon the basis of his famous 1965 Howard University address. The point was formalized by the economist, Andrew Brimmer, in the 1966 edition of *The American Negro Reference Book* edited by John Davis (Englewood Cliffs, N.J.: Prentice-Hall, 1966). Brimmer, later a Governor of the Federal Reserve Board, showed that the income was increasingly more maldistributed among non-white than white families. Neither these early uses nor later economic critiques of the idea are cited by Wilson, though reference is made to two later unpublished papers on the subject by Brimmer.

What is new, however, is the notion that this increasing stratification within black America somehow necessarily signals the declining significance of race. None of the many writers who have drawn attention to this phenomenon ever advanced this conclusion. Certainly, these observers viewed the growing variance as indicating the changing significance of race. But neither the phenomenon itself, nor the data cited by Wilson, reveal any decline in the importance of race as such. Indeed, only two of the book's fifteen tables are relevant, for they combine class and race effects on unemployment (Table 11) and on parental presence with own children (Table 15). These tables show strong main effects for both the class and race variables, moderate interactions and no evidence of the "declining significance of race" whatsoever.

The fallacy seems to lie in the belief that an increase in the predictive power of one set of variables (class) necessitates a decrease in the predictive power of another set (race). Others interpret these same data to mean that, while social class as a main effect is increasing for economic outcomes, the class and race interaction terms are also increasing and race as an important main effect persists. Thus, the black poor are far worse off than the white poor and the black middle-class still has a long way to catch up with the white middle-class in wealth and economic security. Black median family income is not closing the gap with white median family income even with the growing disparity within black America.

To be sure, Wilson hedges on his conclusion. He admits that it applies only to the economic sphere. He knows that white resistance continues to rage against residential integration, public school desegregation, and black control of central cities, — all signs of "*the unyielding importance of race* in America" (p. 152, [emphasis] added). But these "antagonisms," he insists, are far less, historically and individually, crucial for access to opportunities than economic antagonism. This counter assumes relative independence of economics from the "sociopolitical" sectors of life—an unwarranted assumption in the light of the sociological literature, generally, and the racial discrimination literature, in particular. Wilson, himself, implies these connections when he stresses the economic consequences of the current concentration of blacks in declining core cities.

Therefore, I believe that the chief conclusion of this volume— *The Declining Significance of Race*—to be premature at best, dangerously wrong at worst. The unqualified title attracts attention to the book. But it unwittingly risks adding unsubstantiated support to the dominant ideological myth of the current "post-Reconstruction" phase of American race relations: namely, that racial problems were basically solved during the 1960s and, thus, there is no continuing need for such measures as affirmative action and metropolitan approaches to public school desegregation. In fairness, Wilson does not make such arguments; in fact, I am certain that he would repudiate them forcefully. But in the politically charged arena of race relations, his misleading title has already been exploited by conservative spokesmen.

Preferable to the present volume, then, would have been a book entitled "The *Changing* Significance of Race" that spelled out the author's theoretical ideas in detail.

Chapter **10** ON THE DECLINING
— AND INCREASING —
SIGNIFICANCE OF RACE

Charles Payne,
Northwestern University

The reaction to William Wilson's *The Declining Significance of Race* may tell us more about the state of the sociological art and about the state of American race relations than will the book itself. Hailed in some quarters as a signal contribution to the literature, the work is being blasted elsewhere with the charge that it is thoroughly distorting in content and probably reactionary in its consequences. That the reactions themselves seem motivated partly by racial considerations is more than mildly ironic.

We may think of Wilson as developing two interlocked but distinguishable arguments. There is a general theory which divides American racial history into three stages and argues that the patterns of racial conflict and dominance in each period are shaped by changing conditions in the economy and polity. This is in distinction to those theories giving primacy to one or the other. There is also a special theory which applies the principles of the general theory to the modern era in such a way as to lead to the conclusion that the significance of race is declining, an unhappy phrase by which Wilson apparently means something like this: the extent to which whites self-consciously and overtly use race as a means to suppress black life chances, as measured by income and occupational distribution, has declined, while the significance of social class background among blacks for the same outcomes has increased to a point where it is now more important than race.

Although it takes some interesting side-trips, the main business in the earlier part of the work seems to be the attempt to understand the economic basis for nineteenth-century racism, which comes to mean an attempt at assessing the relative value of the orthodox Marxist and the split-labor interpretations of the question. By the first — and labeling anything "orthodox Marxist" is certain to fuel an argument — Wilson refers to the position that racism is directly attributable to the profit-motivated manipulations of an economic elite. On the other hand, the split labor approach (Bonacich 1972–1976) traces racism to the attempts of a relatively well paid and economically powerful segment of the working class to protect its position against the threat posed by the existence of cheaper labor pools. Both of these are materialist theories, of course. Aside from a short discussion of racial belief systems which raises some pointed questions about the conventional interpretation of the influence of industrialization on race relations, Wilson is primarily concerned with determining what type of materialist theory best fits that part of our history, giving just slight attention to non-materialist possibilities.

From the antebellum period until some point shortly after the Civil War, Wilson takes the system of production as his dominant factor. The simplicity of the division of labor made white workers marginal, insuring the economic hegemony of the slave-holding aristocracy, which they were able to translate into political hegemony as well. Race relations, under these circumstances developed a paternalistic quality, i.e., they involved specification of reciprocal duties and rights. Wilson is careful about distinguishing his position from the more extreme treatments of paternalism — classically Elkins (1959) — which focus on the presumed tendency of slaves to internalize the system's norms. It is the period that Wilson finds the clearest evidence for the orthodox Marxist interpretation.

Industrialization changes things in some important ways. In the last quarter of the century, the first stirrings of industrialization in the South improved the economic position of poor whites, enabling them to institute the Jim Crow system as a means to minimize economic competition from blacks. Thus, Wilson says, a split labor market theory becomes more readily applicable.

These changes don't affect the role of the polity in any essential way. In either period, the polity operated basically as reinforcement for patterns of racial dynamics generated by economic factors. It is in the more industrialized North that Wilson finds clearer evidence for his claims about the autonomy of the polity. After something of a honeymoon period just prior to the turn of the century, race relations, there, came to be dominated by economic competition, with the antagonisms reinforced by competition in the social order, particularly by competition over housing. (Note that competition for housing has become "social," i.e., non-economic.) Here, however, the political system remained neutral, neither reinforcing racial stratification nor mediating racial conflict. To assume a more active role, politicians would have had to put themselves against either the interests of industrial owners or those of white workers.

Throughout this discussion, the principles of general theory are restated in the form of calls for greater theoretical eclecticism, for greater historical specificity in the application of theory, and warnings against static, one-variable analysis. This is probably the most significant contribution of the work, but the execution is less than satisfying. The discussion of the antebellum period treats the political hegemony of the aristocracy as a given, as if how a small, land-holding class manages to politically neutralize a much larger, generally, enfranchised group should be self-evident. The discussion of post-war industrialization in the South is similarly uninformative. Despite some brief illustrative comments drawing primarily on the work of C. Vann Woodward, there is really little here that one could call a discussion of the issue. At best, we are left with a vague sense of the extent and pace of the process, of the evidence suggesting that industrial job competition had consequences different from those associated with the agricultural sector, and of the means by which the, presumably, improved economic status of white workers led to increased political resources. It is, certainly, not immediately clear that the skill requirements of some of the industries mentioned in passing—turpentine, textiles, tobacco factories—are such as to create a class of skilled workers indispensable to the production process. Wilson does refer to the greater ease of organization associated with industrialization but that point, also, is not discussed in any detail, so that this discussion is no more satisfying than the treatment given to the same problem by Marx in the *Manifesto*. The pervasive lack of depth in this segment of Wilson's argument stands in sharp contrast to the detail and precision of his discussion of the migration from the South, a discussion which is only background since it raises no issues either empirically or theoretically problematic.

This is all the more perplexing since it is not obvious that Wilson needs to raise the issue of industrialization at all. The line of reasoning that he seems to want to pursue does require that poorer whites have a sense of racial threat but the situation in the post-war South certainly offers several possible bases for that other than industrialization, possibilities that Wilson treats parenthetically or ignores.

In the end, what have we learned about the utility of a Marxist as opposed to a split-labor theory of racial inequality? Less than one might think. In a summary statement on page 60, he repeats his feelings that the Marxist explanation "is restricted" to the antebellum period and the years immediately following the war while the split-labor theory "can only be used to explain racial stratification in the late antebellum North and the origins of Jim Crow segregation in the postbellum South." On the same page, also in reference to the Jim Crow system, he says:

> The racial caste system ... was solidified both by the
> ruling class' support of disfranchisement and by the
> working class' drive (with tacit approval of the rul-
> ing class) toward racial exclusiveness in occupation,
> education and political power.

If one maintains that the post-war ruling class supported disfranchisement, worked to divide the working class along racial lines (p. 54) and, at least, tacitly approved of the drive toward racial exclusion, one has already conceded the spirit if not the letter of the economic elite thesis. What seems called for is some compromise between that thesis and the split-labor theory.

Turning back to the analysis of twentieth-century race relations, we have already alluded to the fact that Wilson sees the central dynamic there as the way in which class conflict between white workers and white management produced racial conflict between white and black workers while hamstringing the polity. As blacks were increasingly absorbed into the unions, particularly in the wake of New Deal legislation, the basis for racial antagonism was significantly reduced. Nevertheless, this did not translate into greater black access to the ethnically controlled political machines, depriving blacks of the "politicization of ethnicity" experienced by other groups, i.e., of the use of ethnic patterns and identity as the foundation for interest-group politics (p. 81). In consequence, the prewar political style of urban blacks was dominated to an unusual extent by a middle-class elite since the absence of integration with the machines also meant an absence of pressures that would have forced vertical integration of the elite with the black masses.

Thus, Wilson's argument about the racial neutrality of the polity prior to WW II is intended to apply only to the national political structure. To the extent that the courts sanctioned restrictive covenants, separate-but-equal policies and the like throughout much of this period, the argument should be narrowed further still. More importantly, Wilson's summary statements concerning the machines, again, seem difficult to reconcile with his description. He said both that "... this racial oppression had no direct connection with or influence on race relations in the private industrial sector" (p. 149) and that it meant blacks were excluded from patronage jobs and government contracts and services (p. 85). Unless we adopt a stringent definition of "direct connection" — and it is not certain that we ought, given Wilson's purposes — the two statements are, at least, potentially at variance. Near exclusion from one of the avenues of mobility that had been significant for other groups implies that blacks were relatively more dependent on the private industrial sector and that, certainly, should have had some implications for the quality of race relations within that sector, however indirect.

Here we have a lesser example of one of the greater problems in Wilson's analysis, the problem of interconnections. How shall we conceptually separate the economic category from others? How direct need a connection between categories be before we define it as relevant? Wilson's failure to adequately handle these questions bedevils his entire analysis, including his attempt to demonstrate the autonomy of the political system after World War II.

The attempt is straightforward enough. The weakening of political machines and the increasing size of the black urban population in the North enabled blacks to exert increasing pressure on government, reflected in more progressive policies from Washington in the 1940s. Ultimately, under the impetus of the civil rights movement, the federal government embarked on policies designed to promote racial equality, much in contrast to its racial neutrality prior to the war and its tendency to support racial inequality prior to the turn of the century.

Wilson can fairly be accused of sketchy characterization here. A case can be made that during the same period, the federal government pursued housing, urban development, and transportation policies that worked disproportionately to the disadvantage of blacks. What Washington giveth with the one hand, it taketh away quietly with the other. Still, relative to its role in earlier eras, Wilson's characterization is within reason. The explanation is more questionable.

First we have to raise some empirical questions about the significance imputed to black voting power. Wilson has no discussion of the evidence suggesting that the increasingly progressive policies coming out of Washington after 1940 were responses to changes in voting power. Alternative explanations are certainly possible. One might argue, for example, that in the wartime atmosphere the threatened possibility of massive demonstrations by blacks became a more potent tool. Then, too, if black votes were so important nationally, we might reasonably expect that they were also important locally. Some discussion of that would have added to Wilson's case. Finally, many of the more important changes in federal policy were initiated by the judiciary, often to be greeted with indifference or hostility by the other branches of government. Presumably, the judiciary is the branch of government least likely to be responding to the pressure of votes.

It is the problem of interconnection, though, which is really interesting. If we grant Wilson's argument, have we learned much about the autonomy of the political system? If racial policies were becoming more progressive in response to increasing black voting power, that voting power itself was a response to demographic changes having fundamentally economic roots. The political repercussions of economic needs appear to be a poor basis on which to establish the autonomy of the political system. Of course, we can write off that argument by saying that the economic influences are entirely indirect. Perhaps that is a reasonable response, perhaps not. The point is, how do we decide where to draw the line?

Perhaps the most convincing way to argue for political autonomy would be to show the political system successfully moving in one direction despite economic forces pressuring it in some other direction. This is precisely what Wilson is not arguing. The entire thrust of his case is that, as we move into the postwar era, the economic basis for racial exclusion is eroded; eroded for white workers by the changes attendant upon the integration of unions; eroded for management by the development of labor practices which made it increasingly difficult to replace troublesome white labor with cheaper black labor. These are Wilson's own arguments and, given them, it would seem that the most he wants to say is that weakening the economic motive for racial ineqality is associated, whether causally or not, with parallel changes in political policy, all of which seems to call for some summary conceptualization short of "autonomy."

Despite his eclectic intentions, Wilson seems, in the end, to be primarily an economic determinist of the narrower sort. This is only, partly, a matter of arguments, advertised as non-economic, turning out to be only a step or so removed from economic roots; and only, partly, a matter of conceptual inadequacies making it difficult to follow some of his distinctions. It

is largely a matter of Wilson losing contact with the possibly independent effects of racial belief systems, a point receiving little
development after his discussion of the mid-nineteenth century.
More broadly, Wilson clearly wants to move the discussion beyond
the familiar level of cultural and psychological factors by
highlighting structural features of the economy and the polity.
We could do with a great deal more of that but Wilson goes too
far. Moving beyond the level of social psychology means adding
to it, not leaving it out altogether.

Suppose we grant the proposition that, for most of this
century, the most important racial tensions have been generated
by economic competition. Still, even if one generation learned
to hate and to act on that hatred on the shop floor and the picket
line, didn't their children learn the same lessons earlier and
elsewhere? The dictum of the social psychologists which holds
that attitudes toward other groups are learned more through
contact with the prevailing attitudes toward that group than
from contact, competitive or otherwise, with that group is given
much less attention than it deserves in Wilson's analysis. Taking
the analysis as a whole, I think it fair to say that Wilson is reducing racism to economic and political rationality channeled by
systemic restraints. This seems just about as sophisticated as the
old attempts to reduce it to the irrationalities of culture, personality, ignorance; that is, the work is ahistorical despite the
historical format.

Conceptual inadequacies show up with greatest clarity in
the special theory, the part of Wilson's argument which sets the
declining significance of race in post-WW II America. That
discussion is predicated upon his very efficient discussion of certain structural shifts in the American economy and the role of
blacks within it. The war pulled significant numbers of blacks
into manufacturing jobs but economic changes following the war
shifted the emphasis of the national economy from manufacturing to service. The lack of expansion in the goods-producing
sector meant a decrease in the number of desirable job options
open to lower-class blacks. In addition, technological changes
made many unskilled workers simply redundant, particularly in
an economy where changes in compensation patterns and work

rules often make the cost of blue-collar labor more a function of the number of workers employed than of the number of hours worked. Thus, even when demand for labor is high, employers may find it cheaper to pay overtime than to hire more workers. Finally, in the face of protective union legislation and equal employment legislation, it becomes all but impossible for employers to use blacks as a kind of reserve industrial army. In consequence, the significance of race in labor-management strife is nearly eliminated while lower-class blacks, more because of their class position than because of their racial background, find themselves locked into the unstable, marginal, and lower-paying jobs.

For blacks with more education or training, the situation could hardly be more different. Affirmative action programs, especially in areas where labor demand exceeds labor supply and, more importantly, the growing availability of white-collar positions in the public sector, have created a vastly more favorable job market for educated blacks. As a result, we may expect a growing gap between them and the black under-class.

Wilson's discussion of the changing connection between race and the economy may not say very much that is new but it does offer a provocative interpretation of well-known information. It would be possible, though, to add another dimension to it. In the 1940s, Ralph Ellison (1953:299) suggested that the introduction of Northern-style race relations to the American South would make possible the more efficient exploitation of the region's social and economic resources. Since then, of course, what was once the Northern mode of racial interaction has become the national mode and we have witnessed immense growth in the Southern economy. Whether there really is, as Ellison expected, any connection between the two is still very much an open question, open because we have given little thought to the possibility. Hopefully, we can pay more attention to it as we continue to explore the kinds of questions which lead Wilson to conclude that the significance of race is declining.

We should be as clear as we can about what that phrase does not mean. Wilson does not mean that the consequences of historical patterns of racism have no significance in the contemporary world; he is quite aware that the dead past lives with us yet, if less than clear about how to fit that into his theoretical scheme. Nor is he saying that contemporary racial discrimination is nonexistent or negligible. There is, I think, an almost natural temptation to respond to Wilson by citing recent studies attesting to the continuing vitality of discriminatory patterns but to do so quite misses his point. Nor is he denying that people continue to use race as a highly salient, often emotional, basis for social identification. He is not even saying that racial tensions are less intense than they once were, only that they have shifted to less important areas.

We have already alluded to the fact that it is not easy to draw a distinction between race as social identity and race as economic determinant or between the more important and less important categories of racial conflict. A study done a few years ago by Mark Granovetter (1974) illustrates the problem well. Looking at career patterns among a sample of professional, technical, and managerial workers from the Boston area, Granovetter's findings support what most of us have long suspected: access to jobs, particularly to the better paying and more satisfying jobs, depends heavily on personal contacts. So long as race is socially salient contact networks will continue to develop primarily within racial groups so that social life and economic life should continue to intersect in some important ways even in the absence of overt racial discrimination.

The point of this is not to say, "Aha! Your categories are not mutually exclusive. They interpenetrate!" Of course they do, and we expect some conceptual ambiguity in an ambitious work. It is because of that ambiguity that we want to take special care in the development of typological schemes. The need is all the greater, in this case, because Wilson is using category labels which are so familiar that one can easily be seduced into thinking that their conceptual content needs no elaboration. Careful elaboration ought, at a minimum, give us some idea about how to think about the boundaries between categories and some idea of why the boundaries should be drawn there. Wilson is not doing this. He is not, for example, giving us any clear discussion of what he means by "sociopolitical order," although whatever it may be, we do know that it includes conflict over residential and school desegregation and over urban political resources. This is definition by example. Moreover, these examples seem to involve conflict over certain kinds of life chances, economic life chances in part. If that is so, do we really need a distinction between them and the other life chances that Wilson puts into his economic category, whatever he may mean by that? (My best guess, incidentally, is that for most of the argument, Wilson is conceiving of the economy as job acquisition and the machinery related to it, not as, say, control over productive resources or as consumption patterns.)

If Wilson tells us little about what his categories mean he tells us more about why some of them are more important than others, thereby justifying the contention that the significance of race is declining even while racial antagonism remains high. High though antagonisms may be in the sociopolitical order:

> ... such antagonism has far less effect on individual and group access to those opportunities and resources that are centrally important for life survival than antagonism in the economic sector. The factors that most severely affected black life chances in previous years were the racial oppression and antagonism in the economic sector. (p. 153)

He, then, goes on to say that even sociopolitical antagonism is not sociopolitical in its origin since " ... the ultimate basis for current racial tension is the deleterious effect of basic structural changes in the modern American economy ...." which is, of course, a materialist interpretation, a curious ending for a work purporting to demonstrate the limited utility of a Marxist paradigm.

We may wonder whether the issue here is really "life survival." We might note as well that Wilson has only the most indirect evidence for the proposition that sociopolitical conflicts have economic roots but let both points pass. What is more important at the moment is that the argument is simply confusing. If racial antagonisms remain strong, if they continue to express themselves in battles over life chances, if those battles have ultimately economic roots, what purpose is being served by this residual category of the sociopolitical order, a category that, generally, seems to mean little more than "non-economic?" The distinction which, at first, seems self-evident and harmless begins to appear increasingly arbitrary. If all Wilson wants to say is that certain important outcomes of racial antagonism have become much less predictable than previously, that is all well and good and it is, certainly, important but making that point requires neither this awkward conceptual trapping nor the conclusion that the significance of race is declining.

Conceptual awkwardness expresses itself in another way. Wilson uses terms like racial antagonism, racial conflict, tension, discrimination, and oppression as if they were interchangeable. Whether they are so, obviously, depends on how one chooses to define them; but as commonly employed, these terms may tap quite different dimensions of interracial interaction. Treating them as synonyms muddles certain fundamental distinctions between the subjective and the objective, between process and consequence, between form and content, leaving us with an omnibus conceptualization of racial nastiness.

Let us return to the issue of creeping materialism. Despite the presumed shift of antagonism from the economic to the sociopolitical order, Wilson argues (p. 116) that "... the key actors on the racial stage remain the same," i.e., lower-income whites and lower-income blacks. Both groups feel the full impact of the urban fiscal crisis, of increased crime, poorer services, and poorer schools and "Thus, the racial struggle for power and privilege in the central city is, essentially, a struggle between the have-nots."

This seems to call for some response. The interpretation seems rather uncritical for a work concerned with assessing the utility of a Marxist paradigm, a paradigm which implies that when we find working class racial antagonisms we ought to consider the possibilities that they are, ultimately, expressions of class relationships. Similarly, Wilson's assertion, here, that the working class have always been the key actors seems at variance with the arguments given in the earlier part of the book. Such a statement would have appeared more reasonable, for example, if he had not devoted a previous section to a fairly extensive discussion of the extent to which the industrialists of an earlier era orchestrated racial antagonism. Here, again, the analysis and the description seem to proceed along independent paths.

His discussion of black/Jewish hosility comes close to suggesting a different interpretation of the class basis of modern racial antagonism. In the aftermath of Bakke, it does not seem unreasonable to suppose that recent changes in racial patterns have created a more realistic basis for racial antagonism among socially privileged whites than had been the case in earlier years. It is my impression, at least, that increasing numbers of upper-middle whites in many sectors of the economy see black economic progress as immediately threatening and as, fundamentally, unfair.

Suppose we accept, for the moment, the contention that racial strife is now essentially a struggle between have-nots. His earlier discussions, of course, tend to portray racial strife as an element in the struggle between haves and have-nots. Such a change would lend itself, among many other possibilities, to the interpretation of racial strife which sees it as either a proxy of or a safety valve for tensions generated by have/have-not class relations. The racial hostilities of white workers prevent their pursuing questions of class as aggressively as they, otherwise, might. If we are looking for a peg upon which to hang a Marxist interpretation of contemporary racial relations, we could hardly hope to find one more obvious.

As if to redress the balance, Wilson seems to become almost too Marxist, in his subsequent discussion of the civil rights movement, imputing to the class factor even greater weight than it deserves. Although he has a different view of the end of the decade, his position is that "Lower-income blacks had little involvement in civil rights politics up to the mid-1960s." Insofar as Wilson wants to say that the leadership of the early non-violent resistance movement was disproportionately middle-class and that that fact affected the nature of the movements in important ways, fine. Equating that, however, with "little lower-class involvement" borders on the preposterous. The history that stretches from Montgomery to Selma is—possibly above all else — a history of the politics of class collaboration. Had lower-class blacks actually had little involvement in the movement, the movement, simply, would not have been. It was they who filled the streets and the jails, stayed off the busses and tested the prohibitions against voter registration. All of this was done at the direction of an elite, assuredly, and relations across class lines were often uneasy, certainly; but to leap from that to the proposition that the lower classes had little involvement is to make a mockery of the historical record and to lose one of the real keys to understanding subsequent tensions in American racial politics. Perhaps Wilson means to say that lower-class involvement was more episodic than middle-class involvement which would be more defensible.

Wilson's contention that the movement ultimately proved most beneficial to those blacks already highest in the scale of social privilege is another matter altogether. Probably, he should have noted that, to the extent that the movement addressed itself to the destruction of the institutionalized symbols of racial stigma, it had important consequences for blacks, irrespective of class background. Beyond that, the point is well taken, especially with reference to its economic consequences.

What is striking, here, is that Wilson can ascribe the improved economic circumstances of many blacks to this history of racial politics in large measure and, yet, go on to talk about the declining economic significance of race. Does that mean that the politics were non-racial or non-significant? Interpreting the consequences of race-conscious activity as proof of the declining significance of race is ahistoricism of the first order, on a par with taking the creation of the State of Israel to herald the declining significance of Judaism. Precisely what seems to have happened is that blacks have become increasingly skilled at using racial identity to political and economic advantage, at using it as protective cloister, as lever, a process Wilson calls the politicization of ethnicity when it occurs among other groups. It is in this sense that we can argue that race has become increasingly significant not only as determinant of black life chances but as a determinant of white life chances as well and many whites seem more aware of this than Professor Wilson.

There is a possible objection here. Isn't much of this simply a problem in semantics? Wilson persists in talking about "the declining significance of race" when, in fact, he clearly means to say racism or economic racism or, better still, the declining effectiveness of job market racism. Had he used one of the latter, less grand, phrases, would not much of the confusion have been prevented and would not the reactions to the work have been less extreme?

No. This line of reasoning will not answer at all. One has to suspect that the problem cuts much more deeply than less felicitous phrasing. There is, I maintain, a long tradition in American scholarship which refuses to see, in the phenomenon of race, much more than unmitigated misery and unchanging impotence. It is nearly always the case with Wilson that, in summary analytical statements, what is central about race, for him, is the way in which whites use it, self-consciously, as a tool of suppression. How blacks use race becomes an issue in some of his descriptive statements but only there. No matter what language one chooses, it seems dangerous for a work whose main business is untangling the webs that tie race to life chances to proceed from so one-sided a vision of racial processes. Some of the better recent works on race are founded upon a much more complex view of the problem. With all due respect for the empirical quality of Gutman's analysis of the slave family (1976), what makes the work instructive is primarily its angle of vision, the fact that Gutman compliments the familiar query, "What did slaves do with what was done to them?" The same sense of race as a two-way process undergirds Levine's (1977) work on black folk culture or, to reach back some, Ellison's criticisms of the social science of his day (1953). At this juncture, any work remaining insensitive to these varied warnings takes us a long way backwards and it is largely by remaining insensitive that Wilson is able to come out at "the declining significance of race."

But even if the interpretation of the process is less than satisfying, is not his description of that process more or less accurate? That is, is it not reasonable to assert that the extent to which whites self-consciously, overtly and successfully use race as grounds for limiting black access to the job market is decreasing, even though we may balk at equating that with the declining significance of race? Well, yes, that is more than reasonable. Saying that, however, is just not news these days and is, hardly, entitled to all the fanfare. Indeed, the matter has already been approached from other theoretical perspectives. For some time, now, we have been hearing about institutionalized discrimination. Defined in various ways, the concept is, almost invariably, associated with the argument that race continues to be a salient element in stratifying processes despite the fact that it is not used as overtly nor as deliberately as before (Knowles and Prewitt: 1969; Carmichael and Hamilton: 1967; Butler: 1976). I find the literature developing this theme open to question on several grounds but it seems improper for Wilson to proceed as if it did not exist. Doing so, undeservedly and, no doubt, unintentionally, gives his work an air of revelations newly received.

What is new is the argument that class has become more important than race but nothing in Wilson allows us to choose that interpretation over the interpretation suggested by the institutional discrimination school. Wilson is not purporting to actually measure the relative impact of class and race on black life chances. More, excepting the discussion of the changes in the structure of the job market, he can be quite vague about the nature of these impersonal class barriers, a point to which we need to give closer attention and a point which takes us back to the adequacy of his conceptualization.

Mr. Wilson is quite aware that discrimination in residential housing is still common, a point verified by a recent HEW study (Eggers, Reid, et al: 1978). That, he writes off, as a sociopolitical matter. Aside from being questionable categorization on its face, the problem with that, given the recent tendency for new jobs to be located away from residential concentrations of blacks, is that any restrictions on residential choice may easily translate into restrictions on job access. Moreover, restrictions on residential choice, presumably, make the perpetuation of inferior inner-city schools more likely, opening a fresh can of worms for Wilson, since his arguments about impersonal class barriers attach substantial importance to the low educational credentials among poor blacks. Despite several references to the poor quality of inner-city schools, he treats the matter as if bad schools in the ghetto simply drop from the heavens as if we can be sure that nothing racial is operating there. That, to put it as mildly as possible, is premature.

Wilson's position becomes reasonable if we accept model inner-city schools centering on either IQ deficits or cultural deficits but not if we adopt the models centering on teacher expectations (e.g., Rist: 1977). The latter argument attaches educational outcomes to teacher expectations and there is some reason to believe that these expectations are generated, in part, by race. Persell's review of the literature (1977:103–5) reports seven studies suggesting such a relationship. One would not want to generalize from the samples used, however. Persell cites two studies finding no such relationship and we certainly cannot yet be certain that teacher expectations really do influence educational outcomes in any important way. With all of this admitted, it is sufficient for our purposes to note that we are hardly in a position to conclude that race plays a negligible role in schooling, which is to say that we are hardly in a position to characterize schools as impersonal, class barriers.

We can put the possibilities in more general terms. It is entirely possible, given what we now know, that the processes sustaining differentials in racial privilege have become a good deal more fragmented than they once were. Where previously the transactions sustaining racial hegemony were, largely, deliberately racist interpersonal transactions, supported by institutional sanctions, now the pattern tends to be one in which racial decisions made in one institutional context and, perhaps, made without malice, have implications in other contexts, including the economic one, which serve to sustain racial inequality. Insofar as the process is fragmented across institutional boundaries and, thus, stripped of some of its interpersonal and emotional character, we may speak of the rationalization of inequality in much the same sense that we speak of the rationalization of work. Wilson's data are too gross to offer a test of such a model but nothing in his argument suggests that a model of this sort could not be applied to the changes which concern him and a model centering on fragmentation is quite consistent with some of the assumptions we normally make about the distinctive quality of social relationships under conditions of modernity. Additionally, such a model leaves open the fascinating possibility that race not only continues to operate as a sorting out mechanism but that it does so, given its fragmented and non-emotional quality, in a fashion relatively unlikely to generate grounds for focused resentment. Thus, the response to the politicization of race may consist of concessions which are likely to be depoliticizing in their consequences.

Drawing on the same tradition, we would also expect a shift in the relative importance of ascribed and achieved status criteria. This does not mean that ascription suddenly becomes irrelevant in the world but it does mean that we would no longer expect to find the extremely high correlations between ascriptive characteristics and life chances that we often find in the pre-rationalized world. For the present problem, this would mean that class should become more important in some respects, while race continues to be salient to different degrees in different interactional contexts. Above all, such a model, rather than making arbitrary distinctions among social categories and trying to assess their relative importance, implies that it is the interplay among the categories, the connections in a fragmented process, which are most important.

On balance, what shall we make of this work? We have, here in its general theory, a work which wants to look at the intersection of race and life chance as a changing, evolving phenomenon. We have a work which refuses to leave the analysis at the attitudinal level, which warns us against overcommitment to any single paradigm. Few academics since Franklin Frazier have reminded us so forcefully that the American racial experience has been a highly variegated one and is rapidly becoming more so.

We also have a work seriously flawed in execution, sketchy in its historical treatment, somewhat awkward and narrow in its conceptualization, just plain careless in its language, seemingly self-contradictory in part, holding to a rather simplistic view of racial interaction which is neither thoughtful nor thought provoking. It is, despite the disavowals, a work which holds so rigidly to a single theoretical viewpoint throughout most of the argument as to jettison whatever relevant lessons are to be gleaned from several decades of social psychological work. The insensitivity to alternate explanations and to the limitations of the data would, by themselves, suggest an unbecoming lack of intellectual humility but attempting to address these questions in one hundred and fifty-three pages is nothing short of hubris. In short, what we have, here, is neither uninteresting nor unpromising taken as a first draft but it constitutes rather an indifferent book.

Any summary judgment must remain arguable. Grant me this one, momentarily, for the sake of allowing us to speculate very briefly on the meaning of the reactions to the book, since the judgment, if roughly accurate, would imply that there is nothing in the content of the work to justify either the uncritical praise coming from some audiences or the unrelieved criticism coming from others. Even if it did not seem slightly dishonest to proceed as if that question did not hover over all of this, we might suppose that any theory which convincingly explicates the changing nexus between race and economics will necessarily shed some light on these reactions as well. The one, as much as the other, seems to have something to do with the increasing politicization of race. We have to presume, that is, that the reactions reflect something more than just the usual differences in professional judgment and even something more than that selective perception which leaves the privileged or those somehow identified with them ready to perceive the arrival of the millenimum in every minor change while those whose world views are shaped elsewhere tend to see partial change as mere palliative, as a potential excuse for no further change.

We might expect that the tradition of equating race with degradation and impotence would eventually generate its own counterdynamic but the more important factors seem to have come from outside the academy. The politicization of race meant that it was invested with increasingly moral and antagonist overtones and more and more associated with the idea that change is a matter of privilege giving up something tangible, not a matter of privilege softening its heart and issuing soothing pronouncements of goodwill. Thinking about race in such an atmosphere becomes threatening and unsettling, perhaps more so for academics than for most others. Wilson offers a way out. Why, it's not race after all; it's just plain, old class. The sigh of relief at the thought that maybe now they will stop waving the bloody shirt is all but audible. Similarly, the vision of Wilson's harshest critics may be affected by their fear of losing an ideological weapon. Should that be the case, chances are that the weapon they fear to lose is one which has already lost its potency, more now a comforting anachronism than anything else.

Be that as it may, though, the depth of the disparity of judgment about this work suggests that the dialogue of the deaf will be with us a while longer.

REFERENCES

Bonacich, Edna. 1972. "A Theory Of Ethnic Antagonism: The Split Labor Market." *American Sociological Review,* October.

Bonacich, Edna. 1976. "Advanced Capitalism and Black-White Race Relations In The U.S." *American Sociological Review,* February.

Butler, John. 1976. "Inequality in the Military." *American Sociological Review,* October.

Carmichael, Stokely and Charles Hamilton. 1976. *Black Power.* New York: Vintage.

Elkins, Stanley. *Slavery.* 1959. Chicago: University of Chicago Press.

Ellison, Ralph. 1953. *Shadow and Act.* New York: Collier.

Eggers, F., C. Reid, J. Simonson, and R. Wienk. 1978. "Background Information and Initial Findings of the Housing Market Practices Survey." Washington, D.C.: U.S. Department of Health, Education and Welfare.

Granovetter, Mark. 1974. *Getting a Job.* Cambridge, M.A.: Harvard Press.

Gutman, Herbert. 1976. *The Black Family in Slavery and Freedon: 1750-1925.* New York: Pantheon.

Knowles, L. and K. Prewitt. 1969. *Institutional Racism in America.* Englewood Cliffs, New Jersey: Prentice-Hall.

Levine, Lawrence. 1977. *Black Culture and Black Consciousness.* New York: Oxford.

Persell, Caroline. 1977. *Education and Inequality.* New York: Free Press.

Rist, Ray. 1977. "On Understanding the Processes of Schooling: The Contributions of Labeling Theory." In J. Karabel and A. H. Halsey (eds.), *Power and Ideology in Education.* New York: Oxford.

PART IV

COMMENTARY ON THE TRULY DISADVANTAGED

Chapter **11** THE THEORY OF THE
UNDER-CLASS: A REVIEW OF
WILSON'S *THE TRULY
DISADVANTAGED**

Theodore J. Lowi,
Cornell University

The Truly Disadvantaged (TD) is a postscript to William
Julius Wilson's earlier work, *The Declining Significance of
Race* (DSR). DSR had caused a great stir but not because it
focused on the phenomenon of class within race. It had so de-
emphasized race that it became an instrument in the hands of
the anti-civil rights forces. TD seems to be an effort to clarify
the author's purpose.

Wilson, in DSR, was not the first black or white social scientist to bring the factor of class into the study of ethnic or
racial communities. True, Wilson focused on it more relentlessly
than anyone before him and he worked through its features and
its theoretical and practical consequences with an unprecedented
combination of rigor and passion. True, also, there are data,
analyses, and findings worthy of the honor the book received
and sufficient to satisfy a lifetime of ambition to make a contribution to the society as well as to social science. Nevertheless,
DSR casued a stir because it gave comfort to the enemies of civil
rights laws. Two passages will indicate how the writings of a
serious black social scientist could have been seized upon by an-
tagonists for their own purposes:

*Reprinted with permission of the author and *Policy Studies Review,* Summer
1988, Vol. 7, No. 4, 852-58.

With the passage of equal employment legislation and the authorization of affirmative action programs, the government has helped clear the path of the more privileged blacks, who have the requisite education and training to enter the mainstream of American occupations ... the very attempts of the government to eliminate traditional racial barriers through such programs as affirmative action have had the unintentional effect of contributing to the growing economic class divisions within the black community.
(DSR, p. 19.)

I remain convinced that the recent developments associated with our modern industrial society are largely responsible for the creation of a semi-permanent under-class in the ghettos and that the predicament of the under-class cannot be satisfactorily addressed by the mere passage of civil rights laws or the introduction of special racial programs such as affirmative action.
(DSR, p. 166.)

Reaction against civil rights policies and their implementation was far from Wilson's intention as he put the case more clearly in TD. But that was the effect of DSR. It became a kind of Catch 22: civil rights policies, designed for the middle-classes, had succeeded so well that they worked themselves out of a job. The problem remaining was the black under-class and that was best to be handled by economic means in a robust economy where new jobs were constantly being created. But, of course, the best approach to the economy was a deregulated free economy. Thus, in neither the upper- or the lower-income situations were race-specific policies any longer needed. (And, of course, welfare undermines the will to work.) Wilson did not go as far as Sowell or Loury, who argued, in effect, that affirmative action was a curse because it stigmatized any black assisted by it. Think of all those white children of Ivy League alumni whose entire lives were stigmatized because they gained admission despite their lack of qualifications because the Ivy League schools have always had alumni affirmative action programs. Think of all those government employees whose entire careers were stigmatized because, for all of the twentieth century, the government has had an affirmative action program called veterans preference. Although Wilson did not go that far, DSR was drawn into the category of civil rights reactionism.

It seems to me that this is the only way to explain why Wilson would write a book-length postscript to DSR. TD is a whole book about the black under-class; yet, DSR had already devoted sixty of its two hundred eighteen pages to that subject. And the fact that Wilson introduced the concept of the black under-class on page one and page two of DSR indicates he had intended to make the black under-class an essential part of the thesis of DSR. Why, then, a whole new book just on the under-class?

Wilson provides the answer on the first page of the preface of TD: 1. to call attention to the worsening condition of the black under-class by giving it a comprehensive analysis; and 2. to spell out, in more detail than before, the policy implications of the analysis. Perhaps a third part of the explanation was his frustration with the fact that the reaction to DSR was "almost total preoccupation with my arguments concerning the black middle class." All this comes together, I think, around the fact that Gilder (*Wealth & Poverty*) was published in 1981 and Murray (*Losing Ground*) in 1984. Both books could give Wilson and everyone else a sense of where the Wilson-type arguments could be taken. Both the Gilder and Murray books were big best-sellers, not only in monetary terms but also among the conservative elites who were making policies during the Reagan administration.

Although TD does present some valuable new data and, of course, updates the situation with the black under-class in the nine years since DSR was published, nothing in TD advances the concept any further or changes the theoretical argument in DSR about the black under-class, except, perhaps, the shift to a more dramatic label for them, "the truly disadvantaged." But that points precisely toward the underlying motivation for TD. A strenuous effort was going to be necessary for Wilson to escape his bondage as a servant to conservative social policy and one place to begin was with a bound off the rhetoric of President Reagan, who so often promised not to turn his back on an undefined group bearing that name, "the truly disadvantaged." It is a throwback to the nineteenth century concept of "deserving poor," as distinct from the "undeserving poor." It is deeply conservative in the sense that the question of truly or deserving was to be left to the judgment of the holder of the resources, whether a private philanthropist or a public agency, in contrast to the liberal, twentieth century approach which tends to leave more of the decision of dependency up to the dependent persons themselves. I, myself, wish Wilson had drawn his inspiration from Thorsten Veblen and had entitled TD "The Theory Of The Under-Class." The ironic rhetoric of Veblen is so much better than the stigmatic rhetoric of Reagan. But no matter, a long article or a revised second edition of DSR would have been sufficient if updating and emphasis were all that Wilson had been seeking. What he was seeking, in fact, was a proper empirical premise for a new direction of policy discourse. One fact distinguishes TD from DSR and this is the fact premise of the whole argument of TD: The black under-class and its continuing decline is not a function of the escaping black middle class or of welfare. It is a function of the joblessness of young black males: that explains their poverty and their non-marriageability and that, in turn, explains the decline of family and the perpetuation of a black under-class as a "culture of poverty." True, this fact situation is exacerbated by isolation from middle-class role models and middle-class stability and by the eligibility of unwed mothers for welfare. But the root cause is joblessness and the culture of poverty that perpetual joblessness produces.

Wilson reports that he tried to make this argument first in a long article in 1985 but was almost completely misunderstood in the popular media, which focused on the exodus of the black middle- and working-class members of the ghetto. The media also focused on the contribution of Southern origins to the perpetuation of urban poverty when, in fact, Southern-born blacks, who migrated to the northern ghettos, experienced greater economic success than those blacks born and raised in the northern ghettos (p. 55). Wilson's correction of the misreading of his first effort deserves quoting at length:

> The key theoretical concept ... is not culture of poverty but social isolation (p. 61) ... Long-term joblessness [excludes young blacks] from the job network system that permeates other neighbor-hoods and that is so important in learning about and being recommended for jobs ... [and] girls who become pregnant out of wedlock invariably give birth out of wedlock because of a shrinking pool of marriageable, that is, employed, black males .... The net effect is that joblessness, as a way of life, takes on a different social meaning; the relationship between schooling and post-school employment takes on a different meaning. The development of cognitive, linguistic, and other educational and other job-related skills necessary for the world of work in the mainstream economy is thereby adversely effected.... A vicious cycle is perpetuated through the family, through the community and through the schools (p. 57). [Thus] the recent trend among scholars and policy makers to neglect the role of male joblessness while emphasizing the role of welfare is especially questionable (p. 63).

We should have known all this before Wilson had to remind everyone who had misread DSR. Take an eloquent excerpt from Oscar Handlin's classic as one example:

> Under the disorganizing pressure of the [ghetto], men found it difficult ... to determine what their own roles should be .... [I]n the peasant world the person who did not earn his own bread was not fully a man, lost thereby status and esteem in the eyes of the community .... [I]n America, pauperism was not

sought out; it came itself to good and wicked alike. No blame could attach here to him who could not always earn a livelihood, who came to depend for his sustenance on the gifts of charity.

Almost without self-pity and altogether without reproach, they surrendered to the institutions that maintained the dependent or they abandoned their families or they became not quite permanent clients of the relief agencies.... Others yielded in a different way — pauperism, insanity, intemperance, gambling.... It was significant of such deviations ... that they represented a yielding to the disorganizing pressure of the environment. These men did not step out of their roles as sober, industrious, thrifty breadwinners as a means of defying society, as a pure act of will. They deviated out of compulsion. (Handlin, *The Uprooted*, pp. 156-62.)

If Handlin's moving words fit all uprooted men, why do we need concepts such as "culture of poverty" and "under-class" for the ghettos when occupied by blacks as when we did not need such concepts when the ghettos were occupied by Jews or Irish or Italians or non-Jewish Poles or others? For the others, George Gildner is correct that there is a dynamic within groups, such that significant numbers of individuals within those groups are mobile even if the groups themselves "have been at the bottom for centuries ..." (George Gildner, *Wealth and Poverty*, p. 12). But, as Wilson has amply demonstrated, Gildner's observation is not true for blacks, and it seems to me it is disingenuous of people like Gildner to oppose government civil rights and welfare policies on the grounds that there is ample individual mobility already. The answer to the question about the need for such concepts as culture of poverty is, of course, the pure and simple fact of racism. Blacks have remained under-class as a group. Race prejudice the world over is stronger than ethnic prejudice and, in America, race prejudice has meant prejudice against Afro-Americans. Wilson should have entitled his first book *The Increasing Significance of Class* rather than *The Declining Significance of Race;* and, although I do not know Professor Wilson personally, I would bet after reading TD that he might well agree with me about a retroactive change in the title. Wilson is quite correct in his observation that liberals avoided such terms as "culture of poverty" like the plague and for the same reasons that conservatives embraced it. It permitted its users to blame poverty on the poor themselves, their lack of character, their lack of ambition, and their inferior cultural traditions.

This brings us to the finale. Class is up and race is down? Would that it were true as a guide to public policy. Class may be up but what is down is not race but American shame toward lack of progress in reversing the disadvantage of race in America. Having seized on the aspirin that class and the economy are now the problem, Americans were able to relax their shame about race. Wilson went far in TD to take away the aspirin and correct that misapprehension. But when he moves on to public policy, he is a good deal less successful.

Wilson begins his policy analysis appropriately with recognition that the first period of policy toward racial problems, 1950–1970, focused on the individual and individual rights. He concludes with the lament that this proved good as far as it went but was quite insufficient, mainly because "the principle of individual rights" does not address "the substantive inequality that exists at the time the bias is removed [and] may linger on for indefinite periods of time after racial barriers are eliminated" (p. 113). Step two in the policy history, beginning around 1970, focused on "the equitable distribution of *group* rights, ... government-mandated affirmative action programs designed to ensure minority representation in employment, in public programs, and in education" (p. 114, emphasis in original). The purpose of affirmative action programs is to negate the effects of past discrimination. But, according to Wilson, the most advantaged minority members profit disproportionately from the benefits of these policies just as they profit disproportionately from the more conventional civil rights policies that focus on individual rights.

Having determined that phase 1 and phase 2 policies are inadequate and insufficient for the task of dealing with the truly disadvantaged, Wilson turns to the work of political philosopher James Fishkin for a third alterantive:

> ... the principle of equality of life chances ... [i.e.] a
> person should not be able to enter a hospital ward of
> healthy newborn babies and, on the basis of class,
> race, sex, or other arbitrary negative characteristics,
> predict the eventual positions in society of those
> children. (Fishkin quoted on p. 117 of TD)

Policies based on this third principle would not be applied restrictively to defined racial or ethnic groups but "would be targeted to truly disadvantaged individuals regardless of their race or ethnicity" (p. 117). Drawing further on Fishkin, Wilson argues that this principle does not "require any reference to past discrimination as the basis for justification" (quoting Fishkin, p. 117). It is based purely on economic-class background and would not only help poor whites but also would be more effective in reaching the poor blacks. Moreover, it would have the advantage of not causing political friction between the white poor and the poor of other racial or ethnic backgrounds. For example, since removal of racial barriers is useless unless "positions are available ... to enhance social mobility," the proper policies would focus on the modern economy and the creation of appropriate jobs (p. 122).

But if all of Chapter 5 is devoted to establishing that point, Wilson immediately sees a special problem and devotes Chapter 6 to that: The special case of the "war on poverty." Wilson claims that the war on poverty failed because its goal was to give the disadvantaged the income and skills they needed but did not "change the economic rules in their favor." That is to say, the war on poverty involved a "separation of anti-poverty measures from national income policy" (p. 130). This, of course, played directly into the hands of people like Charles Murray. In brief, it became "difficult for liberals ... to explain the sharp increase in inner-city poverty, joblessness, female-headed families, and welfare dependency since 1970 without reference to individual or group deficiencies" (p. 132). Since Wilson had already established unemployment and under-employment as the key to the problem, it was logical to go on to argue that the only answer was to be found in the structure of the economy itself, to redress the recent structural shifts that have hit minorities the hardest: relocation in the suburbs (far from ghettos), the shift away from basic industry (where minorities do best) to services (where pay is lowest) and the shift from hands to heads (giving favor to education generally unavailable to minorities). So, according to this, "culture of poverty" should be replaced with the concept of "social isolation" and policies should be aimed accordingly.

The policy part of the book is an anticlimax; and maybe it is true of all bold analyses to disappoint their most ardent supporters. What Wilson is recommending is a program of social democracy that may be a sound of joy to all liberals. Basically, he is arguing for restoration and, perhaps, a bold extension of domestic economic policies that democrats have always favored and may, once again, be in favor with the American public after 1989. But there is more to fear in this than mere anticlimax. It is quite possible that a decade of such social democratic programs will be discredited just as the decade of civil rights and affirmative action programs was discredited by the persistence of the worst features of the ghettos. Has anyone over the age of forty forgotten the original Kennedy response to the demand for civil rights laws: heat up the economy with public works, investment tax credits and defense policies. "A rising tide lifts all boats." It was seen in the early 1960s as a cop-out that required the 1963 March on Washington. Maybe it is true that the time is now ripe for what Wilson calls a "universal reform package" (p. 157), but people in the early 1960s feared that no matter how much you heat up the economy, you cannot reach the really poor.

The social democratic agenda will fail to reach the truly disadvantaged because it does not address racism. And Wilson seems to agree because, despite the support for a "universal reform package," he makes "no claims that such programs will lead to a revitalization of neighborhoods in the inner city," but can only express hope that "in the long run these programs will lift the ghetto under-class from the throes of long-term poverty and welfare dependency ..." (pp. 157-58). But, then, he finds himself forced back to the approaches that more directly address the ghetto, as, I think, is inevitable. At this point, Wilson waffles, moving among several proposals that would, otherwise, be unacceptable to him except for the fact that they have the virtue of combining liberal and conservative approaches. For example, although he is deeply critical of "workfare," as representing no fundamental shift from traditional American approaches to the deserving poor and to the stress on individual character, Wilson ultimately embraces a "new-style workfare." He does not develop the idea beyond a quote from its author, claiming that the new-style workfare "takes the form of obligational state programs that involve an array of employment and training services and activities — job search, job training, education programs, and also community work experience" (quoting Richard Nathan, on p. 161 of TD). But Wilson already gave reasons in TD why workfare will not work.

If a return to social democracy is favored by a majority of Americans, they are likely also to accept a "group benefits approach," a redistribution toward specifically defined groups (i.e., blacks) and specifically defined problems (i.e., group disadvantage). If properly explained to Americans, they will accept it because they already have experiences that prepare them for acceptance. I mentioned earlier our experience with benign quotas in Ivy League admissions and with positive discrimination or affirmative action with regard to veterans preference. Take the latter, because there is an elaborate defense of veterans preference based upon the same argument that could be made to support explicit group compensation under affirmative action — that people deserve compensation for having sacrificed or having been sacrificed — for the good of the country or because of some evil deed for which the country is responsible. We are all aware that "hard cases make bad law;" the worst thing to do in analysis or in policy is to revise a good category in order to accommodate an exception. It is, for example, true in America that constitutional rights are defined in terms of individuals and not groups. But there is experience in American history for explicitly recognizing an exception to an otherwise good rule and blacks have been so recognized. One can say it all began with the founding itself, by treating blacks as "other such persons," to be counted only as a voteless three-fifths of whites. It was confirmed in the first definitive interpretation of the Fourteenth Amendment by the Supreme Court, which stated explicitly that the "pervading purpose" of the Fourteenth Amendment was to protect "negroes ... *as a class.*" Here is the whole sentence: "The gross injustice and hardship against [negroes] as a class, was the evil to be remedied..." (The Slaughterhouse Cases, 16 Wallace 36, 1873, emphasis added). Why insist on the color blindness of the Constitution only now? Why insist only now that the group approach to rights is an unacceptable violation of constitutional principle? Explicitly and forthrightly making a case for blacks as a historic exception is the only way to reverse history. And, besides, it is good civic training. If we could have twenty-five years of affirmative action, where blacks—or the truly disadvantaged blacks—were, in fact, singled out as an exceptional case of group benefits in order to reverse history, the larger principle of rights as individual matters would, in fact, be restored to such a point that, maybe, we would, then, have the luxury not, merely, of the declining significance of race and the shrinking of the truly disadvantaged but the disappearance of both.

12 REBUTTAL TO A
CONSERVATIVE STRATEGY
FOR REDUCING POVERTY*

Charles V. Willie,
Harvard University

In his study of *The Truly Disadvantaged,* Wilson claims
that he is providing a balanced approach that ultimately may
permit liberal policymakers (as opposed to conservative policymakers) to refocus their perspective and appropriately address
the issues. Calling his approach "balanced" does not make it so.
Also Wilson clearly is a conservative masquerading as a liberal.
Rather than freeing himself of ideology that he denounces in
others, he has presented an analysis of poor black people that is
based on a mixed ideology and, thus, is more confusing because
neither he nor others really know where he stands.

Moreover, the real issues in analyzing the causes of poverty
and in prescribing ways of overcoming it are not mainly respon-
sibilities of conservative or liberal social scientists and
policymakers, as Wilson would have us to believe. The issues
and their resolution require the input of the people who experience the problem of poverty as well as those who do not.
Wilson's prescriptions do not entertain input by the victims of
poverty, presumably, because they are outside the mainstream
of American society, according to his classification.

As he sees it, policy prescriptions are the work of mainstream
analysts, like himself and others, particularly liberal analysts.

---

*Reprinted with permission of the author and *Policy Studies Review,* Summer,
1988, Vol. 7, No. 4, 865-75.

According to Wilson, however, liberals have defaulted to conservatives and discounted themselves as valid policymakers to prescribe for ways of overcoming poverty among blacks because they have avoided describing any behavior that might be classified as "stigmatizing to ghetto residents," and because many simply refuse to use the term *under-class,* calling it a destructive and misleading way of "lump[ing] together different people who have different problems." How stigmatizing or stereotyping any population, including residents of a ghetto under-class can help them, Wilson does not reveal. Thus, he proceeds to do just that — stigmatize and stereotype poor blacks. Wilson has prepared and published a study that, he claims, is for the purpose of helping poor blacks but, actually, is harmful to them.

Wilson's discussion of ideology and his self-identification as a "social democrat" who is "to the left" and who is trying to help "the liberal perspective" to refocus so that it may challenge "the now-dominant conservative views on the ghetto under-class" misses the point of social reform. Those who suffer deprivation must be party to the policymaking discussions of how to overcome it. This principle we learned from the civil rights movement during the era of Martin Luther King, Jr.'s leadership. Even then, social scientists and policymakers during the 1960s tried to ignore the poor and their leaders, as Wilson attempts to do today. It was foolish to do it then, as now. Wilson has committed this folly by designating himself as the policy prescriber for effective ways of dealing with poverty. But his diagnoses and prescriptions are not new and, in fact, are similar to those advocated by Daniel P. Moynihan in the past.

In an essay on "Community Development and Social Change" (Willie 1977: 151), I mention that Moynihan's book, *Maximum Feasible Misunderstanding,* "discusses the so-called war on poverty of the Johnson administration as if it were concocted out of the minds of university professors and as if the main issue was a hassle between the Columbia University and the Harvard University professors about the appropriate way to fight the war." Further, I point out that, according to Moynihan, the Columbia professors won and the war on poverty was lost (Moynihan 1969). Although Moynihan's book was subtitled,

"Community Action in the War on Poverty," he devoted not a single reference to the efforts of the Reverend Martin Luther King, Jr. Moynihan's discussion, like that of Wilson's, ignored the poor and their leaders as having a role in a public policy-making about poverty.

During the 1960s, Moynihan characterized the policymaking debate as a contest between the proposals of Columbia and Harvard professors; now during the 1980s, Wilson characterizes the policymaking debate as a contest between the perspectives of liberals and conservatives. Both are wrong. It is action or inaction from the people of poverty that, ultimately, will influence the policymaking process and lead to an effective or ineffective outcome. Because Wilson insists on classifying the black poor who live in ghettos as under-class outside the mainstream, he, therefore, ignores them.

Also, he asserts that their persisting experiences of racial discrimination are unrelated to persisting experiences of poverty. Some social scientists and policymakers have classified his studies as those of a black analyst today that are similar to those of white analysts yesterday that were inappropriate, not very helpful and possibly harmful because they were flawed in study-design and in the interpretation of data. The Wilson studies do not compare the relative effects of poverty on black and white populations, do not analyze variations in prevalence rates of poverty over the years for racial groups and do not interpret the meaning of changes in these rates.

Again and again, Wilson asserts that the condition of the under-class is worse today than in the past and that there is "sharp increase in social pathologies in ghetto communities" such as long-term unemployment, street crime, aberrant behavior, long-term poverty and welfare dependence. Wilson believes that these pathologies of the under-class "are not captured in the more standard designation *lower-class.*" Without evidence of the prevailing behavior patterns of poor people in the inner city three or four decades ago, Wilson claims that today they "differ markedly" from the past and "contrasts sharply with that of mainstream America." He repeats this assertion so often that one could believe it is based on data, which is it not.

A review of literary and ethnographic studies of the past reveal that the plight of 1930s white dispossessed was not substantially different from the plight of the black disadvantaged in the 1980s. Among the "Okies," about whom John Steinbeck wrote, there was poverty, crime, and aberrant behavior (Steinbeck, 1939). Nor is the poverty, crime, and aberrant behavior of city blacks today substantially different from the "pathologies" in black city ghettos in the late 1930s and 1940s, according to accounts rendered by Richard Wright. His account of black city life then could be labeled a lamentation:

> We watch strange modes fill our children. The streets ... the taverns ... the poolrooms claim them. We cannot keep them in school.... Young bodies ... feel bitter and frustrated at the sight of alluring hopes and prizes denied them.... They go to death on the city pavement faster than disease and starvation can take them.... Our final days are full of apprehension, for our children grapple with the city. We cannot bear to look at them; they struggle against great odds (Wright 1941: 136).

And the sorry state of affairs for city blacks three to four decades ago are not much different from the way of life of poor whites today as reported by Ken Auletta (1982: 158-74). Tucked away among the rolling hills of Preston County, West Virginia are many troubled and troublesome white families. They, too, suffer the pathologies of incest, alcohol, unemployment, frustration, and family violence (Auletta 1982: 160). The poor whites are similar to the poor blacks whose behavior patterns Wilson has described and labeled as an under-class. A comparative analysis, had Wilson undertaken such, would have revealed that across racial groups and over the decades, the way of life of the poor is similar. Also a comparative analysis would have revealed that pathologies of the white and the black poor are found also among the affluent, especially the pathologies of alcohol and drug abuse, incest, and family violence. Thus, the way of life of the black poor is not radically different from the so-called "mainstream."

Thus, the labeling of the poor as an underclass is a political rather than social science category. Janice Perlman commented on the politics of labeling in her prize-winning book about squatter settlements in Brazil. She found that a good number of the truly disadvantaged "support ... law and order, tradition, and private property" (Perlman 1976: xvi). It is a fact that "the poor themselves improvise critical solutions in the short run"; this is creative rather than deviant behavior. By stigmatizing such behavior, Perlman found that the dominant class can manipulate the poor to preserve the status quo (Perlman 1976: 96). In other words, "those in power ... blame the poor for their position because of deviant attitudes, masking the unwillingness of the powerful to share their privilege" (Perlman 1976: 102). Thus, the concept of an under-class radically different from the mainstream that Wilson has adopted and articulated "fulfill[s] the ideological-political function of preserving the social order which generated [the myth]" (Perlman 1976: 246). Finally, Perlman observed that "when social scientists give academic respectability to a world view which conforms with prevailing prejudices and gives policymakers confidence and legitimacy, it is extremely difficult to introduce a contradictory set of understandings into that closed circle" (Perlman 1976: 247). All of this is to say that the fate of the poor is in part related to the society of which they are part. The mainstream embraces the poor as well as the affluent, despite Wilson's pronouncements to the contrary.

Not only has Wilson's analysis given legitimacy to the ethnocentric prejudices of the affluent, that they are the mainstream and all others are deviant, he explains the persistency of poverty by adopting the perspective of whites and of blacks without integrating the different perspectives by indicating their strengths and limitations. My comparative studies reveal that "the white poor blame their poverty on personal inadequacy and bad luck" while "the black poor blame their poverty on the unjust society" (Willie 1985: 279–80). Although he mentions structural changes and "impersonal economic shifts in advanced industrial society" as well as an "economic structure of racism," Wilson also claims that members of the under-class are misfortunate residents of inner-city ghettos because of inferior education and insufficient occupational skills. Wilson acknowledges that structural arrangements have caused poverty among blacks, but he does not indicate why blacks are disproportionately poor compared to whites who, presumably, suffer structural constraints also. And while Wilson indicates that some structural arrangements cause poverty among blacks, he is selective in the structural arrangements he would invoke to overcome poverty. Acknowledging the presence of an economic structure of racism that has been harmful to blacks, he is against race-specific programs to eliminate racial discrimination. In his opposition to structural program arrangements, such as affirmative action, to overcome institutional discrimination, Wilson came close to denying that injustice in the social system keeps blacks disproportionately poor. If, as stated by economist Herman Miller, "the average [black] earns less than the average white, even when he has the same years of schooling and does the same kind of work" (Miller 1964: 21) then why are institutional cures like race-specific affirmative action programs inappropriate ways of dealing with race-specific institutional discrimination that has race-specific effects?

Wilson claims that "many contemporary problems of race cannot be satisfactorily addressed ... solely by race-specific programs to eliminate racial discrimination...." This statement among other things is an apology for the status quo and the extraordinary privileges experienced by the white dominant group. Because of Wilson's black racial identity, his analysis provides a protective cloak for whites who oppose race-specific justice programs in employment and education but who wish to deny that their actions have racist implications. The Wilson analysis is a convenient shield for some whites against such charges.

Not only does Wilson function as an apologist for the dominant people of power who wish to maintain the status quo that favors them and their racial group, he has (as stated earlier) stigmatized and stereotyped poor blacks and has even engaged in a bit of middle-class black bashing. In a society such as the United States that has antipathy for poor whites and "uppity" blacks, Wilson's bashing of affluent blacks has been welcomed today with the same fervor and sponsorship that E. Franklin Frazier's disparagement of middle-class blacks, in *Black Bourgeoisie,* was welcomed in the past (Frazier, 1957).

Wilson states that one of his goals was "to call attention to the worsening condition of the black under-class in both absolute and relative terms by relating it to the improving position of the black middle-class." By suggesting that "the deteriorating plight of the ghetto under-class *is associated* with the greater success enjoyed by advantaged blacks as a result of race-specific programs" (emphasis added), Wilson has posited a cause-and-effect relationship. In effect, he implies that middle-class blacks took all of the goodies of the civil rights movement for themselves. Despite the Voting Rights Act of 1965, which has increased the participation and, consequently, the representation of all blacks in local and state government and despite the fact that Martin Luther King, Jr. was murdered while conducting a demonstration for better working conditions for garbage collectors in Memphis, Wilson claims that new public policies that emanated from the civil rights movement did little for those who are truly disadvantaged. He backs up his conclusion by citing "authoritative statements" by the black economist, Glenn Loury, who claimed that the most dramatic earning gains in income for blacks have been among professional, technical, and managerial workers; and the least gains, among blacks in the lowest occupations. The evidence for these assertions are not provided. In these matters, Wilson's assertions as well as those of Loury (whom Wilson quotes) are contrary to the facts.

When the national distribution of income is analyzed by quintiles, modest gains that were favorable for blacks were observed in both the lowest and highest income sectors. The proportion of blacks in the lowest income quintile decreased from 43.3 percent in 1954 to 39.6 percent in 1977; this was a modest but favorable change for blacks of 3.7 percentage points. And the proportion of blacks in the highest income quintile increased from 5.3 percent in 1954 to 9.4 percent in 1977; again, this was a modest but favorable change for blacks at 4.1 percentage points (U.S. Bureau of the Census 1980: 483). The major conclusion is that neither at the bottom nor at the top of the income hierarchy has there been substantial gains by blacks during a span of years of nearly a quarter of a century.

To test Wilson's hypothesis that income discrimination against blacks is caused by inferior education and not by racial prejudice, I compared the median earnings of poorly educated whites and poorly educated blacks. Adult family members were classified as poorly educated if they had received an elementary school education or less. Controlling for race, poorly educated blacks earned 23 percent less than poorly educated whites in 1982. At the upper end of the educational hierarchy (adults in families who graduated from college), such blacks received 22 percent less income than college-educated whites (U.S. Bureau of the Census 1985: 447). The obvious conclusion is that well educated blacks did not fare any better than poorly educated blacks in relation to similarly situated whites (Willie 1988: 76).

It is shameful that an affluent nation that has the capacity to eliminate poverty continues to tolerate it and the suffering some of its people experience because of insufficient resources to obtain necessary goods and services. This is the base on which Wilson and others should be summoning us to action. We know that since the black poor and the white poor are similar in many ways already discussed, the black rate of approximately one-third of its population can be further reduced since the white rate is now only one-tenth or less of its population. Wilson has led the public to believe that poverty among one-third of the black poulation is qualitatively different from the poverty that existed among whites and is intractable. Wilson suggests this by asserting that behavior patterns of poor blacks are radically different from those of affluent blacks and all whites in general. To the extent that the public believes his argument, it will retreat from the battle to further reduce poverty with the belief, fueled by the Wilson analysis, that some of the methods of reducing poverty in the past will not work today.

Jonathan Kozol is correct in concluding that "the cause of homelessness is lack of housing" (Kozol 1988: 11). Then, he shows that the lack of housing for poor people is a consequence of our public policy that has resulted in a drop of federal sup-

port for low-income housing (Kozol 1988: 12). This drop in support has ocurred during a period when rents have climbed substantially for those in the lowest income sector. Moreover,
Kozol reports that "nearly half of new jobs created from 1979 to
1985 pay poverty-level wages." Changes in these public policies
by the mainstream population would result in changes in the way
of life of the poor.

The error in Wilson's analysis must be revealed before it is
too late. He could contribute to a reduction in our effort to
eliminate poverty the same way that some social scientists
almost derailed the school reform movement by asserting that
family characteristics, rather than schooling, is the key contribution to academic achievement. Clearly, if schools did not
matter, there was no need for the public to invest more funds in
them. Similarly, if the poverty problem among blacks is intractable, why should public and private funds be allocated for more
poverty-reduction programs?

A programmatic alternative based on this kind of thinking
is to spend more money on ways of containing the poor in their
misery where they are rather than trying to help them to overcome. There is evidence from the past that the idea of containment of blacks has crossed the minds of some public officials.
Such an idea is likely to emerge again, especially if given
legitimacy by a brilliant, black social scientist. Back in the 1960s
when blacks were rioting in ghetto communities, Gallup pollsters
surveyed blacks and whites and asked what could be done to
prevent civil disorders in central city ghettos. White dominant
people of power listed better law enforcement as the number
one priority, while black subdominant people of power said
that the provision of more and better jobs was the best way to
prevent riots. Despite the fact that most riots occurred in black
ghettos, the nation acted on the white priority by reducing funds
for summer jobs and increasing allocations for the training of
the national guard in riot control methods (Willie 1977: 153-54).
Based on Wilson's analysis of the causes and cures of poverty
among blacks, a response similar to that for containing riots
could be tried and might successfully derail any momentum the
antipoverty movement has achieved todate. For this reason, his

characterization of the behavior of the black poor as qualitatively different from the behavior of people "in the mainstream" is dangerous and may have ominous and evil consequences for poor blacks and all blacks.

I have suggested earlier in this discussion that Wilson's self-designation as a social science planner and policymaker (especially one who is trying to refocus the "liberal perspective" as part of the decision-making process) is inappropriate. Here I wish to declare that his orientation differs so radically from that of poor blacks and other oppressed people that his participation in the policymaking process, supposedly, as one with intimate knowledge of them is harmful. Wilson is a black apologist for the status quo and the white dominant people of power. He reveals this orientation in his crusade against race-specific policies which, in the end, are the only poverty reduction policies that will work.

Just as reducing funds for summer jobs and allocating more money for training the national guard in riot-control methods was an inappropriate public policy for dealing with poverty in the 1960s, de-emphasizing targeted programs for blacks and other oppressed groups, in general, and for poor blacks and other impoverished racial minority populations, in particular, are inappropriate ways of dealing with poverty in the 1980s and in the 1990s.

By stating that his "hidden agenda is to improve the life chances of groups such as the ghetto under-class by emphasizing programs in which the more advantaged of all races can positively relate," Wilson reveals his inadequate knowledge of the history of social reform movements and indicates that he is a proponent of the "trickle down" theory of economics.

Wilson embraces an idea set forth by Lester Thurow that members of the middle class are willing to share some of their income and jobs with those less fortunate than themselves in periods of great economic progress. Thus, Wilson's policy prescriptions would require the poor to wait until the total economy has expanded so that they may obtain the enlarged heap of "scrapes" that the affluent voluntarily share with the poor.

It is truly surprising that such a policy would be advanced by a black social scientist who lived through the civil rights movement during the era of Martin Luther King, Jr. There is evidence that affluent whites with "plenty of something" did not share their excess opportunities with poor blacks and other racial minorities who had "plenty of nothing" until required to do so in specific ways by the court. Public education is a case illustration. Inequality in educational opportunities for racial groups in America did not move toward equity until required to do so as a court-ordered remedy. More than three decades after the historic Brown decision of the Supreme Court that found segregated education "inherently unequal," the United States still has not experienced full desegregation of public schools because the language of the remedy was general and not specific. When a particular or specific group is denied a universal or general opportunity, a group-specific remedy is the only kind that will be effective. This is true for restoring civil rights in government as well as for enhancing academic achievement in education. Group-specific approaches are the only kind that are guaranteed to work effectively.

The social science principle of asymmetry is one on which the group-specific remedy is based. According to this princple, the method of overcoming evil must be asymmetric to the way that evil is expressed. Martin Luther King, Jr. understood this principle well and counseled participants in the civil rights movement in the 1950s and 1960s to use soul force to overcome physical force. Soul force or nonviolence is asymmetrical to physical force or violence.

Philosopher John Rawls deals with the issue of group-specific or person-specific approaches in his discussion of the principle of redress. In compensating for undeserved inequalities, Rawls states, "society must give more attention to those ... with less favorable social position" (Rawls 1971: 100). Society can do this only by way of group-specific or person-specific remedies.

In an earlier chapter, I stated that

... because racial discrimination has been identified as a key cause that keeps blacks at the bottom, it could very well be that different hypotheses are needed for explaining the continuation of poverty in the two racial populations.

Further, I state that

... failure to explore the possibility that different explanations of poverty may be required for different racial populations, which have had essentially different experiences, may have contributed to the contemporary controversy.

Then, I suggest that poverty among poor whites who are less than 10 percent of their population may be due to "motivation, aspiration, and [a fatalistic] life orientation" while poverty among poor blacks who are more than 30 percent of their population may be due to "racial discrimination" and "institutional oppression." My reason for offering differing hypotheses for the different racial populations is because of their different social experiences. For example, I assert that institutional changes during the past three to four decades have resulted in a substantial reduction in the proportion of whites who are poor and that, since external changes in social organization have upgraded nine out of every ten whites, the few who remain poor may reflect those with more personal problems less susceptible to mass institutional amelioration. But the proportion of poor blacks, three out of every ten, is sufficiently large to merit further effort at reducing their poverty through institutional means like affirmative action, antidiscrimination laws and employment programs. Until group-specific programs are put in place and effectively implemented, "we cannot know how large the residual proportion of black poor might be who may need such individualized attention as [that now possibly required for] the few whites [who are poor]." Thus, group-specific programs are needed to deal with the poverty manifested among different population groups because of their different existential experiences. William Wilson does not understand this and has, therefore, advocated universal, nonrace-specific approaches that are wrong.

Finally, I advocate population-specific approaches to the matter of further reducing poverty (and am opposed to the doubt that Wilson casts on this approach) on the basis of political science theory and public health practice. If poverty in the lower-class or under-class is as intractable as Wilson has suggested that it is, we may need to fractionate the problem into its component parts. It has been demonstrated that when the whole problem is too much with which to deal, fractionating it and dealing with a portion of the problem sometimes helps us to get a handle on how to help.

Public health professionals concerned with infant mortality have realized that "as the total rate decreases, the proportion of deaths attributable to different causes may increase," thus requiring several hypotheses to account for the infant mortality that remains (Willie 1962: 526). The same may be said of poverty that has been substantially reduced over the years. No longer may a single effort, such as an expanded economy, substantially reduce what now is a relatively lower rate of poverty. The residual rate probably results from multiple causes and different circumstances and requires population-specific approachs to further reduce the rate that remains.

REFERENCES

Auletta, K. 1982. *The Underclass.* New York: Random House.

Farley, R. 1984. *Blacks and Whites.* Cambridge, M.A.: Harvard University Press.

Frazier, E. F. 1957. *Black Bourgeoisie.* New York: The Free Press.

Kozol, J. 1988. *Rachel and Her Children.* New York: Crown.

Miller, H. 1964. *Rich Man, Poor Man.* New York: Crowell.

Moynihan, D. 1969. *Maximum Feasible Misunderstanding.* New York: Free Press.

Perlman, J. 1976. *The Myth of Marginality.* Berkeley: University of California Press.

Rawls, J. 1971. *A Theory of Justice.* Cambridge, M.A.: Harvard University Press.

Steinbeck, J. 1939. *The Grapes of Wrath.* New York: Viking Press.

U.S. Bureau of the Census. 1980. *Social Indicators III.* Washington, D.C.: U.S. Government Printing Office.

U.S. Bureau of the Census. 1985. *Statistical Abstract of the United States.* Washington, D.C.: U.S. Government Printing Office.

U.S. Bureau of Labor Statistics. 1980. *Handbook of Labor Statistics.* Washington, D.C.: U. S. Government Printing Office.

Willie, C. V. (1962, August) "Racial, Ethnic, and Income Factors in the Epidemiology of Neonatal Mortality." *American Sociological Review,* 27: 522–26.

Willie, C. V. 1977. *Black/Brown/White Relations.* New Brunswick, N.J.: Transaction Books.

Willie, C. V. 1981. *A New Look at Black Families.* Dix Hills, N.Y.: General Hall.

Willie, C. V. 1985. *Black and White Families.* Dix Hills, N.Y.: General Hall.

Willie C. V. 1988. "The Black Family: Striving Toward Freedom." In J. Dewart (ed.), *The State of Black America 1988.* 71-80. New York: National Urban League.

Wright, R., and E. Rosskam. 1941. *12 Million Black Voices.* New York: Viking Press.

Chapter **13** ARE NON-RACE-SPECIFIC
POLICIES THE KEY TO
RESOLVING THE PLIGHT OF
THE INNER-CITY POOR?*

Harold M. Rose,
University of Wisconsin-Milwaukee

Few persons would deny the need for an effective public
policy that would minimize the severity of the social dislocations
currently in evidence in the nation's larger inner-cities. The
question posed here is: can an effective policy best be formulated in a non-race-specific format, as suggested by Wilson
in *The Truly Disadvantaged: The Inner City, The Under-class
and Public Policy* or will the public policy of necessity be forced
to confront, head on, the dire conditions in which a growing
segment of black Americans live? But before we attempt to address
the central issue, a number of substantive points raised in the
book require review.

Wilson provides a clear description of the worsening plight
of the black inner-city poor during the period 1960–80. He chiefly
attributes the deterioration in the quality of life to the structural
transformation of the national economy. This is a frequently
overlooked explanation, as conservative social scientists prefer
to base their explanations on the shortcomings of ghetto residents. According to the author, liberal social scientists since the
late sixties, on the other hand, have essentially withdrawn from
attempts to explain the complex outcomes and increasingly show

*Reprinted with permission of the author and *Policy Studies Review,* Summer
1988, Vol. 7, No. 4, 859–64.

signs of acceptance of conservative arguments. A growing number of black scholars writing for mainstream audiences also appear to be drawn toward the conservative pole. Black scholars manifesting a traditional liberal orientation are said to exhibit a tendency to attribute the behavioral outcomes that Wilson describes as indicators of social dislocation to current racism. Wilson rejects that position. Thus, Wilson perceives himself to be stepping into the vacuum created by the behavior of the previously identified elements of the intellectual community relative to the plight of the so-called under-class.

There are those who consider this an unwise precedent as the promoters of an under-class imagery tend to support a conservative ideology (Macnicol 1987). Yet, he appears quite willing to accept the challenge of responding to conservative scholars whose tendency is to blame the growth of the under-class on the persistence of a culture of poverty and/or the liberal social policies inaugurated by the civil rights movement and Great Society programs. He concludes that liberal scholars tend to be apologists for under-class behaviors while their black counterparts are busy denying the existence of ghetto pathology. The author, no doubt, has stepped into a hornet's nest as many intellectuals are likely to respond negatively to such an assessment. Yet the Wilson view, in some ways, transcends concern with the perspective of those supporting one ideological position or another and is, instead, a bold effort to establish his own position on these issues. He makes it quite clear in the initial chapter that his earlier work, *The Declining Significance of Race,* had been misunderstood. Therefore, one anticipates this work will set the record straight; that a clear picture of the current state of the black inner-city poor will be presented, that a reasonable explanation will be provided of how this state emerged, coupled with a set of prescriptions possessing intellectual merit and the potential for widespread public acceptance.

Wilson should be given high marks for his delineation of the forces that account for the simultaneous movement of blacks out of poverty and the push of another segment of that population deeper into a hole from which escape appears difficult. His treatment of the transformation of the national economy and its impact on black joblessness is well thought-out and commands attention. His macroview of the changes impacting on the inner-city poor during the previous twenty years establishes a theoretical context within which to view the plight of the inner-city poor. But it is at the macro-scale that his assessment shows weakness.

The most glaring weaknesses are those associated with a lack of precision in identifying the primary elements of his investigation. For instance, I am still uncertain who the truly disadvantaged are. Furthermore, it seems that the label "under-class" was chosen more as a means of language synchronization than as a means of illuminating the problem. Although this terminology is becoming part of the American lexicon, it still lacks precision. It should be noted, however, that the precision employed by Ricketts and Sawhill (1988) in defining the underclass is an improvement over ealier definitions that border on the anecdotal (e.g., Auletta, 1982; Lemman, 1986). Nevertheless, the author mounts a vigorous defense in support of the label and asserts that to employ a more neutral descriptor would represent a failure and/or refusal to come to grips with the severity of the plight of the inner-city poor. Even if one agrees with the rationale, based on the author's treatment, it is not easy to identify the magnitude of the under-class population in the nation's larger cities.

Inadequate attention is devoted to establishing the necessary critical thresholds that would permit easy definition of underclass neighborhoods. Instead, we are led to assume that some unspecified level of poverty—out-of-wedlock births, joblessness, and violent crime—reflects the hallmarks of under-class populations. Since the author devotes considerable effort to demonstrate a pattern of black middle-class and working-class abandonment of residential areas that in earlier years were more economically heterogeneous, it can be concluded that under-class neighborhoods are those in which a residual poulation is concentrated. Thus, indirectly, it is possible to deduce from this process the identification of zones of under-class concentration in inner-city areas. But before one moves too far in the direction of attempting to identify the spatial locus of the under-class, it is necessary to make certain that the process described by the author is an accurate appraisal of what has occurred. To begin, it appears that the claims of middle-class abandonment of the ghetto is somewhat overdrawn. Although black professionals participate in a much wider segment of the housing market than ever before, they constitute less than one in six of all black workers. Therefore, one should accept with caution the suggested impact of middle-class abandonment of ghetto neighborhoods as having the suggested impact on emerging under-class behavioral patterns.

One of the strengths of the book is its emphasis on process. Yet in many ways his concern for process gets in the way of the author's addressing some of the concerns previously noted. By focusing on process, the author fails to specify with precision the necessary parameters that distinguish the under-class from other, less marginal, populations. Furthermore, the theoretical support utilized in defense of certain aspects of process are derived from the work of a limited number of scholars. As a result of his drawing upon the work of a narrow band of researchers a number of elements, I believe, critical to the process leading to social dislocation, must be accepted on the basis of faith and intuitive judgment. Nevertheless, in the description of the process, a number of important concerns are developed. None, however, rank in importance with that of the relationship between the male marriage pool and out of wedlock births and selected other social dislocations. Wilson's analysis of the role of macro-economic forces in setting the stage for the growth of the under-class population during the previous twenty years constitutes a rational approach but at the same time too little attention is paid to differences in response to these changes at the level of the local community and/or subcommunity. Are we to assume that the under-class has simply made a passive adaptation to a set of exogenously generated pressures that overwhelmingly account for their present circumstances?

In arguing against the conservatives' tendency to explain social dislocations as a consequence of the belief in the persistence of a culture of poverty, Wilson does not address this problem head on. Instead, he focuses his effort on the declining presence of positive role models as an outgrowth of black middle-class abandonment of inner-city areas. So, indirectly, he does address the role of culture at the micro-scale but in a somewhat oblique fashion. Yet he admonishes other black intellectuals for not being forthright in portraying the character of the problems that permeate inner-city neighborhoods. In my opinion, if one is to devote serious attention to this problem, not only is it necessary to view these problems from a macro-perspective, but from a micro-perspective, as well. The latter would, of necessity, lead one to examine the impact of culture on under-class status in a fashion similar to that employed in an effort to assess the impact of macro-economic change on the adaptive behavior propensities of the target population. A failure to do this places one in a defensive position, where one either argues against the existence of a culture of poverty or attributes the current outcome to the continuing prevalence of racism. Since Wilson rejects the latter, it seems only logical to attempt to assess the role of cultural change, "writ large," on micro-scale behavior if we are to gain a more complete understanding of how these outcomes have evolved.

Wilson should be applauded for his attempt to unravel the complexities of the operation of the American economy and its impact on those whom he identifies as the under-class. Likewise, his willingness to address the growing gap between segments of the black population, based on a differential ability to gain access to those resources that lead to success in the American economy, has, no doubt, partially influenced his advocacy of non-race-specific policies as a means of ameliorating the plight of the black poor. Yet he does not end his effort at this point, however valuable that might have been. He concludes his treatment of the problem by addressing a series of policy options that, he suggests, will aid the truly disadvantaged in overcoming their current position in American society. It is in the area of policy advocacy that this book is most likely to be judged in terms of success or failure. If it fails to contribute to the formulation of policies designed to alter both the life chances and/

or the quality of life of the black under-class it will simply be relegated to the slag heap of intellectual exercises in support of one ideological position over another.

The strategy favored by Wilson is a broad-based policy that would favor job creation, job training, child support, and family allowances targeted at the universe of persons who have been negatively affected by recent structural changes in the economy. Such a strategy is said to have its roots in northwestern Europe. He suggests that a policy of this type would appeal to those who may express opposition to one designed to favor only minority populations at the expense of others. Since such a policy would offer support to individuals across the political and social class spectrum, it would not be subject to the kind of opposition that grows out of policies targeted at the minority poor. Citing the growing opposition of both liberal and conservative scholars to aspects of targeted policies, for example, preferential treatment, a non-work requirement welfare program, he concludes that universally oriented policies are more likely to find support than are targeted policies. Nevertheless, he is aware that secondary targeted policies will be necessary in order to confront current racist practices. While acknowledging this need he fails to provide examples and, therefore, it is unclear where in the scheme of things targeted policies would be located.

On its face, such a policy orientation appears to reflect political rationality and has much to recommend it. Yet as one delves beneath the surface of this "hidden agenda" some of the anticipated promise diminishes. For instance, it is said that such a policy would require the formation of new political alliances. A central question then becomes: With whom should blacks develop alliances given the nature of the social dislocation that such a policy would be expected to address? The author fails to address that question. Furthermore, since the author has appropriately demonstrated the gender-specific attributes manifested by under-class status (e.g., male joblessness, out-of-wedlock birth) how can a universalistic policy orientation aid in addressing such diverse issues? Or, better still, it is possible to form a single alliance that could be expected to foster an effective policy to address gender-specific manifestations of under-class status, or should public policy formation designed to address the under-class plight best be addressed within a family context as suggested by Kelley (1985)? Furthermore, even if one acknowledges the direct link between joblessness, the male marriage pool and out-of-wedlock births, the task of identifying political supporters that would be willing to address these issues in a forthright way, outside of at least a quasi-minority framework, would seem to constitute a Herculean task.

The likelihood of implementation of a nontargeted national policy that would alleviate the social dislocations Wilson describes as pathological, at best, seems weak. Unless such a policy coincides with the development of micro-environmental strategies designed to promote ethnic solidarity, cautious faith in such an effort represents a rational response. The failure of the author to address this issue directly appears to stem from the fear of providing support to those who attribute the current dislocations to the manifestations of a culture of poverty. Given the tendency of both liberal and conservative social scientists to support this notion, such a fear is well founded. I would suggest, however, that the observed negative behaviors that some view as vestiges of a culture of poverty might best be viewed as partial manifestations of a culture of affluence. The culture of affluence prompts that segment of the population with the fewest resources to indiscriminately adopt selected aspects of mainstream behavior without seriously assessing the consequences of their action.

While race-specific policies may fail to gain the kind of support at the national level that has been accorded them in the recent past, race-and/or ethnic-specific strategies will be required at the subcommunity level if the size of the truly disadvantaged population is to diminish. Local populations, in my opinion, are not simply passive entities adapting to macro-economic change as Wilson seems to suggest. The failure to focus attention on what the target population and its supporters might do on their own behalf is one of the major failures of this most recent assessment of the fortunes of the black poor. Yet the policies suggested by Wilson, in conjunction with a series of well-thought-out ethnic strategies, may go a long way towards ameliorating the conditions of the truly disadvantaged. But to think that the kind of macro-economic policy strategies advocated here will turn things around places too much faith in the existence of political partners whose interests in the problem are simply those of eradicating the negative behavior of a segment of the black poor.

The central issue then is not so much the need for a universalistic policy but the nature of this universalistic policy and how such a policy should be expected to interface with a series of race- or ethnic-specific strategies that might best enable the black poor to alter their status. Since joblessness or the absence of adeuqate pay tends to undergird most of the social dislocations highlighted in this work, it seems that greater emphasis should have been directed at those targets. This is not to say that these issues were overlooked but the policy recommendations put forward to overcome these problems were much too vague. It appears that the growing opposition to affirmative action, even in liberal quarters (see, e.g., Jencks, 1985), prompts Wison to advocate a more universalistic-oriented policy approach to the problem. When this is coupled with a seeming belief that former policies primarily benefited the black middle class and is in some indirect way responsible for the growing concentration of the under-class in selected urban neighborhoods, they tend to suggest the failure of race-specific policies to come to grips with the issue.

What becomes acutely obvious in all of this is the continuing belief on the part of the author that the real problems facing blacks at the low end of the stratification system are class-related problems and not essentially race-related problems. The job of untangling the two has indeed become more difficult over time. Nevertheless, as the structural character of the economy continues to change and employment opportunities continue to disperse into white work-ethic zones around the nation, we should be in a better position to test the relative importance of race versus class in establishing barriers to residential and occupational mobility on segments of the black population.

Finally, Wilson should be applauded for again placing the plight of the urban poor black on the national agenda. There is little doubt that this work will stimulate renewed discussion of the issues and out of the ensuing debate there might just emerge a set of policy prescriptions that would, indeed, lead to an amelioration of the plight of the truly disadvantaged.

REFERENCES

Auletta, K. 1982. *The Underclass.* New York: Random House.

Jencks, C. 1985. "Affirmative Action for Blacks, Past, Present and Future." *American Behavioral Scientist,* 28(2). (July/August): 731-60.

Kelley, R. 1985. "The Family and the Urban Underclass" *Journal of Family Issues,* 6. (June): 159-84.

Lemman, N. 1986. "The Origins of the Underclass" *The Atlantic Monthly.* (June): 31-55.

Macnicol, J. 1987. "In Pursuit of the Underclass" *Journal of Social Policy,* 16. (July): 293-318.

Nathan, R. 1987. "Will the Underclass Always Be With Us?" *Society.* (March/April): 57-62.

Pinkney, A. 1984. *The Myth of Black Progress.* New York: Cambridge University Press.

Ricketts, E.R. and V. Sawhill. 1988. "Defining and Measuring the Underclass." *Journal of Policy Analysis and Management,* 7(2): 316-325.

PART V

CONCLUSION

14 ON THE PREVENTION
AND CURE OF
POVERTY AND RACISM

The Willie/Wison debate, toward the end of the twentieth century, has implications for blacks and society at large not unlike those of the DuBois/Washington debate at the beginning of the century. In 1903, W.E.B. DuBois and Booker T. Washington disagreed about the most effective way of overcoming the disadvantaged history of slavery that black Americans had experienced during the nineteenth century and earlier (DuBois 1903; Washington 1903). Washington prescribed industrial education as the pathway to freedom for blacks; he stated that it could be their foundation for commerce, wealth, and ownership of property. Having achieved these, blacks with more leisure, in Washington's opinion, might then look forward to the enjoyment of literature and the fine arts. Ultimately, blacks would not be confined to industrial occupations in Washington's scheme; but, initially, they should learn, for example, tailoring, carpentry, brick masonry, food preparation, and the skills of dairy work. The industrial education that Washington prescribed was for the purpose of preparing students as artisans so that they could obtain occupations which would be open to them in their racially segregated home communities of the South (Washington 1903: 224–25).

DuBois disagreed with the Washington prescription. He believed that a broadly cultured education for black men and women was the quickest way to raise in the scale of civilization a formerly enslaved people. He was annoyed with Washington's ridicule of the teaching of astronomy, theology, Latin, and grammar to blacks. Even industrial training should be taught by broadly educated instructors, DuBois insisted. The day has passed, DuBois believed, when any "wornout" carpenter can teach in a trade school. Such teachers ought to have knowledge of the humanities, sciences, mathematics, and the arts. They needed a broad cultured education, according to DuBois, so that they could teach "life" as well as work (DuBois 1980: 226-28).

DuBois and Washington influenced each other during the course of their protracted debate. Washington conceded that training the hand without training the mind is crude and inappropriate and that there should be no limits to the educational attainment of blacks in arts and letters. DuBois admitted that teaching character and knowledge is of limited value if one has not been taught how to earn a living. He acknowledged that imparting technical knowledge to blacks so that they may learn to work steadily and skillfully is important; but he steadfastly insisted that work alone will not uplift a people. They must be inspired by ideals and guided by intelligence. According to DuBois, these tend to result from education in the arts and sciences and the understanding of modern civilization that they convey.

The debate between DuBois and Washington, during the early years of the first half of this century, was a prelude to the upheaval in educational institutions and the debate about educational reform that has occurred during the second half of the twentieth century. American society would have been better prepared to deal with the issues of educational reform if it had studied carefully the debate between these two educators. In general, American society ignored DuBois and Washington as, merely, two blacks fussing with each other. Because of the minority status of the debaters, the nation did not realize that their analysis had applications for the education and training of the majority group in the society as well as minority groups. Thus, the consensus that DuBois and Washington reached that education ought to teach knowledge, cultivate character, and train individuals to work steadily and skillfully was not incorporated into the curriculum of schools of good learning.

Many educators who had a fleeting interest in the debate considered it only for the purpose of choosing sides with the black whose ideas seemed most closely linked with their own. Without doubt, whites tended to embrace Washington's prescription more frequently; they were less inclined to agree with DuBois.

The Willie/Wilson debate has implications for this nation and whether it will adopt and implement compassionate public policies that embrace affirmative action and the providing of compensating advantages to those who have been unfairly denied opportunities. Again, the nation is inclined to ignore the debate as, merely, that of two blacks fussing. Those who do give fleeting attention to the arguments consider them largely to determine which diagnosis of the persistence of poverty in a society of plenty is closest to their opinion.

Richard Margolis states, Wilson's idea—that "[the] black under-class finds itself the victim, not of racist tradition, but of technological progress," and that the youthful army of unemployed blacks is structurally "an accident of history" rather than a consequence of continuing white discrimination—"has won hands down." He attributes the nod toward Wilson as probably due to the fact that many "are weary of domestic strife and of guilt-edged sermons" and are "eager to accept glad racial tiding with no questions asked, especially when they come to us courtesy of a brilliant black scholar."

The error in Wilson's analysis which leads him to conclude that "economic class" is a more salient determinant of personal life experiences and individual opportunities than is race for blacks in the United States is based largely on his narrow perspective, limited methodology, and inadequate conceptualization of the problem of poverty. Wilson states that his analysis of the relative effects of race and social class is "a macrosociological argument of inequality" (Wilson 1979:159), concerned with providing a structural analysis of racial-group access to rewards and privileges (Wilson 1979:160). Wilson said that his goal was to spell out policy implications that "move ... beyond race-specific policies to ameliorate inner-city social conditions to policies that address the broader problems of social organization, including economic organization" (Wilson 1987: viii).

Wilson does not adequately define micro-units and macro-units of analysis, although his study is presented as a macro-social investigation. Presumably, the mainstream is the macro-unit of analysis. If class is a micro-unit of society, especially the under-class, then all classes are micro-units, including the middle-class as well as the under-class. According to this definition, the under-class is part of the American mainstream. The macro-unit of society is additive as the sum of all of the micro-units. Thus, it is a conceptual error to classify one social class as a micro-unit of society and another social class as a macro-unit. Wilson commits this error by classifying all social classes other than the under-class as the mainstream.

It is important to determine which is micro- and macro- because, by way of a common medium, "the micro-scopic world … [is] inextricably connected to the macro-scopic world" (Lee 1988:28). Moreover, as physicist T. D. Lee has informed us, "the micro-scopic is the basic world and the macro-scopic only its manifestation" (Lee 1988:56). He stated that most of us living in the macro-scopic environment are quite unaware of the micro-scopic world; yet there is union between the two.

As the macro-scopic is a manifestation of the micro-scopic in the physical world, the micro-social is a manifestation of the macro-social in human society. Note that in the physical system, the relationship between micro-units and macro-units is the reverse of what is observed in the social system. The micro-unit is basic in the physical system but the macro-unit is basic in the social system. This fact means that micro-social units should never be classified as deviant or outside the mainstream. They are what they are because of the mainstream—the macro-social unit in whose image the micro-units are fashioned. Because of Wilson's error in conceptualization, he does not acknowledge this fact. As stated by W.J.N. Watkins, "the social whole" …determines matters for the individual that [one] cannot avoid… ." This, he states, is the assumption of some philosophers of history (Knorr-Cetina, 1981:8).

The social stratification system is the mainstream or macro-social unit and all sub-systems are micro-units of it, including the middle-class and the under-class. What happens in these subunits, in part, is influenced by "the social whole." Thus, the under-class and the adaptations of its participants cannot be understood apart from the total social system and the joint effects of all social classes.

Power and its differential distribution is the medium which links the micro-units within a social system. The capacity of micro-units of an economic system, for example, to influence the distribution of rewards and opportunities within the total system is a function of differential power of the various units.

Samuel Bowles and Herbert Gintis state that "overall inequality of income is the sum of inequalities in labor income, inequalities in property income, and inequalities in capital gains." Because of their power "the very same people who receive large property income also are likely to earn substantial labor income and reap large capital gains" (Bowles and Gintis 1976:90).

Lee has characterized the union of the micro-scopic and the macro-scopic as the field of study known as philosophy (Lee 1988:56). A philosophical analysis reveals that this union does not have to work to the disadvantage of any of society's micro-units, including the under-class. Philosopher John Rawls states that the principle of redress is an important element in a theory of justice. It requires compensation for those who have lost out. The principle of redress is a macro-social principle that mitigates the effects of natural accidents and contingencies of history in rewarding opportunities. According to this principle, "no one should benefit from these contingencies except in ways that redound to the well-being of others" (Rawls 1971:100).

The principle of redress is implemented by activating the principle of difference, a micro-social principle which acknowledges the uniqueness of each unit of society such as a social class and attests to its validity. This means, according to Rawls, that society does not have to even out talents or handicaps to be fair.

Since all differences are valid, are held in common and, therefore, benefit or harm the total society, "those who have been favored by nature, whoever they are, may gain from their good fortune only in terms that improve the situation of those who have lost out." This arrangement is necessary, according to

Rawls, because "no one deserves his greater natural capacity nor merits a more favorable starting place in society." Understanding this principle, a society so distributes opportunities that "contingencies work for the good of the least fortunate," and "no one gains or loses from [one's] arbitrary place in the distribution of natural assets or ... initial position in society" (Rawls 1971:101-2). In summary, all are part of the mainstream—the under-class as well as the middle class. None is deviant. Wilson would not have classified the under-class as deviant if he had understood the principle of difference.

Thus, subdominant people of power, including the under-class, have fewer opportunities not because Congress enacted and the White House enforced "sweeping civil rights legislation" as Wilson claims (Wilson 1987:141) and not primarily because of inadequate education but because of continuing injustice in society, especially injustice associated with race, gender, and other characteristics and because of failure of the society to implement the principle of redress.

Discussing Barry Bluestone's analysis of critical institutional and other variables which affect individual labor earnings, Bowles and Gintis report that a male white union member with work experience in the primary segment of the labor market is likely to earn 3.1 times more per hour than a black female worker in the secondary segment. More than half of the difference is due directly to race and gender discrimination; and slightly less than one-fourth is attributable to differential wages associated with primary/secondary labor market segmentation (Bowles and Gintis 1976). These data cast doubt on Wilson's hypothesis that poor education rather than racial discrimination contributes to dislocation among members of the under-class in black ghettos.

That racial and gender discrimination are major contributors to differential income of minority and majority populations was revealed by a report published, a decade ago, by the United States Civil Rights Commission. Using statistical controls that held constant differences in age, education, job prestige, number of weeks worked and region of employment, the Civil Rights Commission discovered that black and other minority males received income that was 15 to 20 percent less than that received by majority white males (U.S. Civil Rights Commission 1978:54).

Less than twelve months now separate black and white adult populations in median number of years of schooling completed. Today, a majority in both racial groups are high school graduates. One could say that blacks are closing the education gap and are beginning to achieve parity in schooling. Yet, as the 1980 decade began, the proportion of professional and managerial workers among white males was nearly twice as great as the proportion of such workers employed as laborers and service workers. The converse was true for black males: their proportion of laborers and service workers was nearly twice as great as the proportion of professional and managerial workers. These differences in employment persist despite an increasing similarity in educational achievement among the races.

Actually, poorly educated blacks earned less than the family income received by poorly educated whites in the United States. The same pattern persisted for highly educated blacks; they earned less than the income received by highly educated whites. Whether one is assessing income differences between the races among the highly or lowly educated a similar gap is found that is associated with their racial characteristics.

William Wilson's perspective limits him to a macro-sociological analysis that ignores the principle of complementarity between the micro-social units of a social system. Also by focusing on the macro-social only, he does not examine and understand linkages between the micro-social and the macro-social and that the micro-social, ultimately, is a manifestation of the macro-social.

Limitations of Wilson's study also are due to its faulty design and methodology which do not facilitate comparative analyses by race and social class, particularly comparative analyses that may hold constant the nominal or the graduated variables.

Beyond these limitations, Wilson's study is impaired because of confusion in his conceptualization of the problems of poverty. By conceptualizing his investigation as a structural analysis, Wilson focuses on spatial features of demarcations. Wilson's method of demarcation labels poor, black people who live in the inner-city as the under-class. While previous definitions of segments of the stratification hierarchy such as lower class and upper class (or even poor and affluent) have a connotation of systemic continuity, the under-class label which Wilson and others have imposed upon poor, inner-city black residents implies systemic discontiniuty and that the under-class is unrelated to the "mainstream." Thus, Wilson's structural analysis has spatialized and isolated the problem of poverty.

The attempt to spatialize the problem of poverty facilitates increased surveillance, political control, and may even target poor, inner-city black individuals for increased discrimination. These possibilities introduce ethical considerations that flow from spatializing a social problem. Wilson does not consider the ethical issue and is more concerned with spatializing the problem for the purpose of formulating public policy. Thus, poor whites who may behave similarly as poor, inner-city blacks but who may reside in rural areas could escape being targeted, discriminated against, and labeled.

Michael Foucault has stated that "A whole history remains to be written of spaces—which would, at the same time, be the history of powers" (Foucault 1977:149). Spatializing the problem of poverty as Wilson has done facilitates the harmful use of power to deny opportunities to the contained population and, therefore, is an ethical problem that needs more study. Wilson asserts that "a fundamental social transformation has taken place in ghetto neighborhoods, that the condition of these residents of inner-city neighborhoods has worsened in recent years." Because Wilson does not understand the power implications of demarcating a people in space and labeling them as pathological and beyond the bounds of "mainstream" society, he has difficulty understanding why it is inappropriate to label poor, inner-city blacks by the term under-class which is a stigma. Wilson seems not to understand that stereotyping poor, inner-city blacks as an under-class that is full of pathology and outside the mainstream gives license to fearful, dominant people of power to control, contain, and constrain such people. By spatializing the problem of poverty in his structural analysis of the urban poor, Wilson is an accomplice to whatever harm is visited upon this population in a deadly "game" of power politics.

In terms of sociological analysis, Wilson's structural approach also blinds him to the need to consider process. In the past, philosophy committed the error of reducing its field to one of process and ignored the structures (Foucault 1977:140). Now sociology and, especially, that brand of sociology represented by Wilson's research has reduced this field of study largely to one that is problematic of structure and ignores process. However, structure and process interact even as space and time are related (Whitehead 1957:3).

To summarize, Wilson's analysis of the interaction of race and social class is defective because he does not define operationally what is micro-social and what is macro-social. He, therefore, is unable to make a proper study of the association between the two, including what is mainstream and what is not. He confuses the analysis by labeling social classes other than the inner-city poor as mainstream and further by labeling the inner-city black poor as deviant. The validity and ethics of this practice are questionable.

Even more serious than the flaws in study design, methodology, and confusion in conceptualization are the policy recommendations that Wilson offers. Wilson believes that the life chances of poor individuals, such as the inner-city black underclass, can be improved "by emphasizing programs to which the more advantaged groups of all races and class backgrounds can positively relate" (Wilson 1987:55). Thus, Wilson rejects population-specific remedies.

Sharon Collins emphasizes the importance of population-specific remedies in her article, "The Making Of The Black Middle-Class." She reports that "the Office of Minority Business Enterprise ... dramatically affected black business' success in selling to the government." She said that, "Fluctuation in minority business sales coincides with changes in purchasing policy." When the Interagency Council for Minority Business Enterprise was created to coordinate all federal purchases from minority firms (a population-specific approach), there was "increased proportion of federal purchases from minority businesses" (Collins 1983:372).

By insisting, as he does, that "economic and social reforms [should] benefit all groups in the United States, not just poor minorities" (Wilson 1987:155), Wilson also rejects the princple of redress. The initiatives that are uniquely those of the dominant people of power in a just society are those of compassion and generosity. Those who have lucked out are obligated to be generous, to give more than they are required in a just and effective society. As Rawls has observed, the principle of redress is for the purpose of providing genuine equality. (Rawls 1971:100).

Wilson's policy recommendations that reject population-specific remedies are wrong also because they are ahistorical. One suspects that his ahistorical approach is due to his over-emphasis on social structure and his under-emphasis on social process. In the 1960s, James Allen, Jr., then Commissioner of Education of the State of New York, credited the efforts taken by school boards throughout the country to achieve quality education for all to the pressure from below, from community subdominants. He testified before the United States Civil Rights Commission that "[blacks] in their demonstrations, in their peaceful demonstrations, have done more than any other segment of our society to push us to the point where we have now gone" (Willie 1977:152-53). Others, including Wilson, have been slow in recognizing that all micro-social units of society, including the poor and the affluent, must be empowered to identify their own self-interests and negotiate with others for mutual fulfillment.

When dominant people of power formulate remedial programs for subdominants, as Wilson has recommended, they are likely to fulfill the interests of dominants first and those of subdominants only after the dominants are satisfied. Wilson's recommendations against group-specific approaches would encourage other groups in the nation to continue to ignore or subordinate the self-interests of the poor to their own self-interests (Wilson 1987:149). Such a policy would be folly.

The United States Civil Rights Commission has compiled new evidence that population-specific affirmative action requirements have improved job opportunities for minorities and women. Major industries such as American Telephone and Telegraph (AT&T) and International Business Machines (IBM) substantially increased the number of minorities in a range of jobs as a result of court orders that required population-specific employment remedies.

Finally, examples that population-specific rather than universal programs of reform are needed as remedies for past discrimination are found in the field of education. Louis Fischer, David Schimmel, and Cynthia Kelly discuss the special rights for handicapped and non-English speaking students. They state that, before the 1980-decade laws, many states did not compel school systems to accept some handicapped students in public schools. Particularly exempt from compulsory school attendance were retarded, emotionally disturbed, deaf, and blind children. Stimulated by the civil rights movement of the 1950s and 1960s, handicapped students and their parents began to press their claim for education in the public schools as a right. This pressure in part resulted in enactment, in 1975, of Public Law 94–142, the Education Of All Handicapped Children Act. Now there are nationwide standards for the education of handicapped children and all handicapped children between the ages of three and eighteen must be provided "free appropriate public education" (Fischer, Schimmel, Kelly 1981:269, 273).

With consciousness also raised by the civil rights movement, immigrant children and their parents organized and asserted their rights. They had to do this because "many teachers had little sympathy for non-English-speaking students" (Fischer, Schimmel, Kelly 1981:270). Litigation in their behalf was necessary to force public education authorities to provide equal educational opportunities for children of limited English-speaking ability by way of population-specific remedies. In *Lau* v. *Nichols* (1974), the Supreme Court declared that universal programs that provide the same facilities, textbooks, teachers, and curriculum for English-speaking students and non-English-speaking students "effectively foreclose [the latter group] from any meaningful education" (Fischer, Schimmel, Kelly 1981:279). The court left the formulation of remedies to educators but clearly stated that a universal approach that did not consider the unique and special needs of students with limited English-speaking ability was inappropriate and even illegal.

Based on this analysis, one may conclude that Wilson's approach to poverty is harmful both to poor people and to the society at large. By spatializing the problem of poverty in his structural analysis as an inner-city phenomenon, he labels poor, urban blacks and places them at risk of containment, constraint, and control by fearful, dominant people of power. By stereotyping poor, inner-city blacks as an under-class, he stigmatizes them and fans the fears of the remainder of the community. By classifying some poor, inner-city black populations as deviant and all others as mainstream, Wilson absolves affluent whites of any responsibility for the way of life of blacks.

While Wilson uses population-specific approaches to label the poor and to describe their behavior, he rejects population-specific approaches in prescribing remedial action. Universal approaches may be helpful in preventing poverty but not in correcting the effects of poverty after it has been experienced. Methods of curing or overcoming misfortune are different from methods of preventing misfortune. Wilson's analysis and policy prescriptions do not recognize this difference.

The poor are placed at risk when their self-interests and special needs are ignored or subordinated as could happen in a universal approach. Since self-interest is the basis for human action, the affluent, the dominant people of power, are likely to fulfill their own interests first in a universal approach. Such an approach is the antithesis to compassion and generosity and is, therefore, unworkable and unworthy. This discussion suggests that Wilson's action-strategy for dealing with poverty and the poor in the United States is wrong. It is not anchored in the accumulated knowledge of ethics and the social sciences.

REFERENCES

Bowles, Samuel and Herbert Gintis. 1976. *Schooling in Capitalist America,* New York: Basic Books.

Collins, Sharon. 1983. "The Making Of The Black Middle Class," 3 (April), 369-82.

DuBois, W.E.B. 1903. "Leadership Education." In Leslie H. Fishel, Jr. and Benjamin Quarles (eds.), *The Black American,* 1976: 226-28. Atlanta, G.A.: Scott, Foresman and Co.

Farley, Reynolds. 1984. *Blacks and Whites.* Cambridge, M.A.: Harvard University Press.

Fischer, Louis, David Schimmel, and Cynthia Cynthia. 1981. *Teachers and the Law.* New York: Longman.

Foucault, Michael. 1977. *Power/Knowledge,* New York: Pantheon Books.

Knorr-Cetina, Karin D. 1981. "The Micro-Sociological Challenge of Macro-Sociology: Toward a Reconstruction of Social Theory and Methodology" In K. Knorr-Cetina and A.V. Cicourel (eds.), *Advances in Social Theory and Methodology.* Boston: Rutledge and Kegan, Paul, 1-47.

Lee, T.D. 1988. *Symmetries, Asymmetries and the World of Particles,* Seattle, WA.: University of Washington Press.

Rawls, John. 1971. *A Theory of Justice,* Cambridge, M.A.: Harvard University Press.

U. S. Civil Rights Commission, *Social Indicators of Equality for Minorities and Women,* Washington, D.C.: U.S. Government Printing Office.

Washington, Booker T. 1903. "The Virtue of Industrial Education." In Leslie H. Fishel, Jr. and Benjamin Quarles (eds.), 1967. *The Black American.* 223-225. Atlanta, G.A.: Scott, Foresman and Co.

Whitehead, Alfred North. 1957. *The Concept of Nature.* Ann Arbor: University of Michigan Press.

Willie, Charles Vert. 1977. *Black/Brown/White Relations.* New Brunswisk, N.J.: Transaction Books.

Willie, Charles Vert. "The Black Family: Striving Toward Freedom." In Janet Dewart (ed.), 71-80. *State of Black Americans 1988.* New York: National Urban League.

Willie, Charles Vert. 1979. *The Caste and Class Controversy.* Dix Hills, N.Y.: General Hall.

Wilson, William Julius. 1978. *The Declining Significance of Race.* Chicago: University of Chicago Press.

Wilson, William Julius. 1979. "The Declining Significance of Race — Revisited But Not Revised." In Charles Vert Willie, *The Caste and Class Controversy,* 159-176. Dix Hills, N.Y.: General Hall.

Wilson, William Julius. 1987. *The Truly Disadvantaged,* Chicago: University of Chicago Press.

Index

Admissions policies, 19–20, 33
Affirmative action, 3–4, 20, 28, 32,
    72, 73, 85, 100, 110, 120, 134–
    35, 139, 141, 149, 165, 170, 177
Allen, James, Jr., 177
Allen, Sanford, 1, 19–20
All Our Children, 15, 72
American Dilemma, An, 96
Antagonism, racial, 122–23
Arrington, Richard, Jr., 66–67
Auletta, Kn, 147

Bakke case, 4, 103
Becker, Ernest, 40, 41
Birmingham, Alabama, 66
Black Codes, 107
Black(s): class divisions, 30–35;
    college educated, 28–30, 71;
    educated and social class, 33–35,
    151; electing, 66–67; family in-
    come, 84–86, 110, 150–51, 173–
    74; family structure, 82–83;
    males, 26, 28–30, 87–88, 136,
    163–64; middle-class, 20–21,
    25, 29, 35–36, 83, 86–87, 98–
    99, 110, 150, 165; occupations
    of, 75–76, 87–88; protest, 104–
    5; underclass, 17, 25, 31–33,
    77, 83, 85, 96, 120, 145–50,
    152, 153, 158–66, 171, 173–76,
    179; voting, 66–67, 104, 118,
    125; women, 30, 49–50, 65, 77
Black Bourgeoisie, 150
"Black Rule in the Urban South,"
    67
Bluestone, Barry, 173
Bonacich, Edna, 107
Boston Globe, 66–67

Bowles, Samuel, 172, 173
Brimmer, Andrew, 35, 104
Bus boycott, 82, 90, 104

Capitalism, economics of advanced,
    32, 98, 107
Changing American Institutions,
    review, 106–11
Cincinnati, Ohio, 69
City University of New York, 103
Civil Rights Act (1964), 69, 77
Civil Rights Commission, 71, 173,
    177
Civil rights movement, 82, 84–85,
    98, 104, 117, 124, 145, 150,
    154, 159, 178
Civil War, 104, 106, 107, 113
Collins, Sharon, 176
Competition, economic, 103, 114,
    119
Conant, James B., 54
Conservatism, 135–36, 144–57,
    159, 161, 164
Corporations, 28–29, 177–78
Courts, minorities and, 70–71, 102,
    116, 150, 178–79
Cox, Oliver, 107
Credentialism, 100
Crime, street, 146–47
"Culture of poverty," 51–52, 136–
    39, 141, 162, 164

Dallas Morning News, 64–65
Davis, John, 109
Declaration of Independence, 95, 96
Declining Significance of Race, The,
    reviews of, 95–100, 101–5,
    106–11

181